MOST HAUNTED

Most Haunted

THE OFFICIAL BEHIND-THE-SCENES GUIDE

Yvette Fielding

AND

Derek Acorah

WITH GILL PAUL

MICHAEL JOSEPH
an imprint of
PENGUIN BOOKS

MICHAEL JOSEPH

Published by the Penguin Group
Penguin Books Ltd, 80 Strand, London WC2R 0RL, England
Penguin Group (USA) Inc., 375 Hudson Street, New York, New York 10014, USA
Penguin Group (Canada), 90 Eglington Avenue East, Suite 700, Toronto, Ontario, Canada M4P 2Y3
(a division of Pearson Penguin Canada Inc.)
Penguin Ireland, 25 St Stephen's Green, Dublin 2, Ireland (a division of Penguin Books Ltd)
Penguin Group (Australia), 250 Camberwell Road,Camberwell, Victoria 3124, Australia
(a division of Pearson Australia Group Pty Ltd)
Penguin Books India Pvt Ltd, 11 Community Centre, Panchsheel Park, New Delhi – 110 017, India
Penguin Group (NZ), cnr Airborne and Rosedale Roads, Albany, Auckland 1310, New Zealand
(a division of Pearson New Zealand Ltd)
Penguin Books (South Africa) (Pty) Ltd, 24 Sturdee Avenue, Rosebank, Johannesburg 2196, South Africa

Penguin Books Ltd, Registered Offices: 80 Strand, London WC2R 0RL, England

www.penguin.com

First published 2005
1

Copyright © Flextech Rights Limited, 2005

The moral right of the author has been asserted

Set in Frutiger and Letter Gothic
Printed in Great Britain by Butler & Tanner Ltd, Frome, Somerset

A CIP catalogue record for this book is available from the British Library

ISBN 9–780–718–14817–7
    0–718–14817–7

Contents

Foreword by Yvette Fielding

As a little girl, I was terrified of the dark; I'm not keen on closed doors and I really don't like being scared – I could never watch something like *The Exorcist*. So how on earth did I end up in a career where I spend the night in the pitch black in properties that are supposedly haunted?

The truth is that I consider myself incredibly lucky to do the job I do. It's varied, I get to travel and meet a lot of fascinating people, and I've always been interested in the paranormal, so I'm getting paid to explore a lifelong curiosity. On the downside, the hours aren't great and I used to have trouble sorting out my sleep patterns in the early days, but I seem to be used to it now.

One of the best things for me is the camaraderie with this amazing group of people, who have become like family. When we spend the night together in a spooky property, our experiences can be totally bizarre. We're all thrown together in this claustrophobic atmosphere, battling with every emotion our bodies can produce. I often compare it with a group of people on a spaceship, or inside a bubble, playing a role in a drama that can seem endless when you're in the middle of it. And

then dawn breaks and we pack up the kit and go home, do the laundry, then drive in to the office. It's a totally surreal way to earn a living.

I don't think I'm particularly psychic. My senses are quite acute and I get teased because it's almost always me who hears strange noises first, so in most shows you'll hear me going 'What was that? Did you hear that?' I also seem to be the one with the strongest sense of smell – which is not always a bonus. Doing *Most Haunted* has been a powerful journey for me, in that I've challenged myself to do things I never would have thought myself capable of, and I'm proud to say that I've come through most episodes without being too pathetic.

This book explains the background to the series – the theories we test out, the methods we use, all the groundwork we put in before the cameras start rolling and our inside accounts of what really happened on some of the most dramatic shoots. There are descriptions of dozens of paranormal incidents that weren't included in the shows that aired, for one reason or another, and, as usual, different members of the team have their individual interpretations of events. We also offer some advice, based on our experiences, to those who want to pursue their own paranormal investigations.

If you've missed any episodes, series 1 to 5 are now available on DVD and you can order your copies from **www.livingtv.co.uk/shop**.

I want to thank everyone who has worked on *Most Haunted*, including all those at Antix, Flextech and LIVINGtv. We are grateful to all the owners who let us film on their properties, the eyewitnesses who were prepared to testify on camera about their ghostly experiences and everyone who has come along to help us at the live events – celebrities and non-celebrities alike. Most of all I want to thank all the viewers who have made the show such a huge success, and I hope you keep watching. There's lots more to come …

Sleep tight!

Introduction
by Derek Acorah

I never wanted to be a medium. I used to call them 'gooks'. My only ambition as a teenager was to play football and, at the age of fifteen, I was lucky enough to be accepted as an apprentice-pro at Liverpool Football Club, under the great Bill Shankly. Sadly, I never made the first team, but I played for Wrexham and then Stockport FC and I thought that football was going to be my life. But my grandmother knew different.

Gran recognized that I was psychic way back when I was knee-high and I described talking to a man on the stairs who looked exactly like her husband, the grandfather who had died before I was born. 'You'll be finished with football by the age of 26,' she told me. 'When you realize it, you'll be in a hot country beginning with the letter A.'

Sure enough, I joined the USC Lions of South Australia League and when I was 26 years old, I sustained yet another injury and realized that I would have to give up professional football. And so I turned to the only other thing I knew I could do well – mediumship.

Over the years, I'd had several visitations from the world of spirits and as I began to do personal readings and sessions in front of an audience in spiritualist churches, I started to appreciate the powerful

gift I'd been given. It was around this time that my spirit guide, Sam, made contact with me. Gran had told me that he would, but it still came as a shock one evening when I was at home alone and this voice said to me, 'Hello Derek, it's Sam.'

We all have spirit guides in this life, whether we are aware of it or not. They are perfectly ordinary people in the spirit world who keep an eye on us. They are there when we are born, then when we leave the physical body, they are waiting to guide us over to the other side. Sam and I first met in Ethiopia more than 2,000 years ago, when I was incarnated as one of five children in a family of poor farmers. Sam – or Masumai, as he was known then – was a traveller we knew, a man of great wisdom for whom I had a lot of respect.

One day, when I was nine, a feud broke out in our village and my mother, father, two brothers and two sisters were all killed in the fighting. I managed to hide in some bushes just outside the village and escape the slaughter, but I was still in shock four days later when Masumai came by. He was to take care of me for the next four years, and I travelled the country with him until I was murdered for stealing a loaf of bread from some tribesmen. As I lay dying in his arms, Masumai told me that I would come back to a new life and that he would be by my side, guiding me. So when he began talking to me that night, I rediscovered a very old, very valued friend, who was to help me with the work that is set out for me on this life's path. We agreed that I should call him Sam now, as it's more fitting in the twenty-first century than an ancient Ethiopian name.

Viewers of *Most Haunted* will be familiar with the way that Sam and I work together. If a spirit wants to get a message across to this world but they don't want to – or aren't able to – talk to me directly, then Sam acts as a go-between. He warns me when spirits are not to be trusted and advises me on how to deal with all the information I receive.

It's not an easy job to do. Sometimes I have thought of quitting because of all the strong emotions and the hurt I encounter, when family members have been murdered or a child lost at birth, or a dearly loved partner has passed over. I have to act as a kind of counsellor, trying to get families to accept that their loved one is not lost and that one day they will meet up again. You have to bring a closure to your sadness and not allow it to take over your life. All the illnesses and disabilities of the physical body are taken away when people pass over to the spirit world and they're back at their prime again, so that's the way you should think of them. When I can use my skills to demonstrate this to individuals who are grieving, it's very rewarding to see how much it helps them.

Sometimes I get information about bad things that are going to happen, and this is particularly difficult to deal with. Even if I warned the person concerned, it would still happen in some way, and I have to be careful because if I ever abuse my power, I could wake up one morning and it would all be gone.

People are always incredulous when I tell them that I know exactly when I'm going to die – in the March of my 84th year. I also know that I'm going to be in a plane crash in my 63rd year, on a flight between the USA and Canada, and I'll be one of only three survivors. But not getting on any planes that year is not the answer – if I didn't, it would just happen in some other way.

I've been communicating with spirits professionally for over 27 years now, and I accept totally that this is my life's path. My mission is to convince as many people as possible that there is life after death, that our consciousness lives on, so when Yvette approached me about being part of the *Most Haunted* team, I knew straight away that I had to do it. I could see back then that after some initial teething problems the show would become a huge success, not just in the UK but also beyond. And I knew that I was meant to be a part of it, to help me reach out to many more people than I would ever be able to talk to face to face.

What I didn't know was quite how much pleasure and satisfaction I would get working with Karl and Yvette and all the members of the wonderful team they've put together. It's disturbing at times, and my aura has been affected after particularly traumatic experiences, but I ground myself by cutting off completely when I'm not at work. I play with my grandchildren, talk to my wife and kids, walk the dogs and every single day I go to my spiritual waterfall and meditate to keep myself whole.

I hope that you continue to enjoy watching the series and that this book sheds extra light on the behind-the-scenes work we all do to make it happen. Wishing you all the very best!

Cast List

Derek Acorah, psychic medium

Karl Beattie, director

David Bull, presenter of live shows

Jon Dibley, cameraman

Richard Felix, historian

Rick Fielding, cameraman

Yvette Fielding, producer and presenter

Jon Gilbert, sound engineer

Craig Harman, steadicam operator

Clare Hollywood, commissioning editor, LIVINGtv

Cath Howe, make-up artist

Wendy James, locations manager

Jason Karl, paranormal investigator

Ian Lawman, psychic medium

Alex Lysaght, locations manager

Sally Matthews, floor manager

Tom O'Carroll, sound engineer

Dr Ciaran O'Keeffe, parapsychologist

Tor O'Neill, production manager

Rachel Philips, script supervisor

Louis Sava, paranormal investigator

Brian Shepherd, psychic artist

Matthew Smith, parapsychologist

Stuart Torevell, chief rigger

Suzanne Vinton, script supervisor

David Wells, psychic medium

Phil Whyman, paranormal investigator

Simon Williams, cameraman

Richard Woolfe, director of television, LIVINGtv

CHAPTER 1

Birth of
a Series

As the twentieth century drew to a close and the twenty-first began, Yvette Fielding was working as a television presenter and her husband, Karl Beattie, was a freelance cameraman. Their ambition was to create a series on their own and they spent a lot of spare time brainstorming ideas, but the spark that was to become *Most Haunted* came from an unexpected direction.

A friend of theirs knew the owner of Michelham Priory, a medieval monastery in East Sussex that had been converted to a private house in the sixteenth century and was filled with beautiful stained glass, tapestries and antique furniture. The friend suggested to Karl and Yvette that they might like to use it as a location for a shoot some time. He finished with a throwaway comment: **'By the way – in case you're interested – it's also haunted.'**

Now Karl and Yvette were both very interested in the paranormal. They discussed what they could film at Michelham Priory, and it was Karl who came up with the idea of spending a 24-hour vigil there, in the dark, with a bunch of paranormal experts of differing degrees of belief and a crew who would express their own responses on camera.

There had been ghost shows on TV before but none had used night-vision cameras, which give that distinctive *Blair Witch Project* feel to the footage – and none had been crazy enough to commit themselves to all-night vigils in locations that had reports of a lot of paranormal activity. Right from the start, Karl wanted to produce a show that was a serious investigation rather than light entertainment, and he wanted it to be about a group of people rather than one or two 'stars'.

One of the difficulties of getting a series of your own off the ground is that no one will advance you the money to make a pilot unless you have a very strong track record – and they won't consider commissioning a series without seeing a pilot. Karl and Yvette were so sure their idea would be a success that they decided to risk their own savings to make it. Yvette approached Derek Acorah, who was also working at Granada Breeze at the time, and explained the plan. '**We'd love you to be involved**,' she said. Derek liked the idea and agreed straight away.

Making the Pilot

The shoot at Michelham Priory was one of the most eventful the team have ever experienced, with lots of paranormal happenings captured on camera – and it was also one of the most scary they would ever do. As soon as they arrived, Derek saw a shadowy 'dark spirit', and the further they progressed into the house, the more they all got the feeling that 'someone' didn't want them to be there. Jason Karl, a paranormal investigator, was getting wildly fluctuating readings on his EMF (electromagnetic field) meter, and the temperature dropped dramatically in certain areas. A huge, sturdy door swung open on its own, then Karl saw the figure of a woman in the kitchen with her legs

Derek and Yvette in the secret tunnel at Michelham Priory.

visible in the fireplace. Derek went down a secret tunnel hidden behind a panel on the stairs, and one of the cameramen took a bad tumble – or was he pushed? Yvette was pinched by a spirit that Derek identified as a young girl called Rosemary and, as they were leaving, the team noticed that a huge chair in the drawing room had moved about a metre forwards into the room. So all in all it was a pretty eventful pilot show!

Back in Manchester, Karl spent several weeks editing all the footage they had amassed, working on his dining-room table because there was no budget for an office, and then at last the tape was ready to show to broadcasters.

Straight away there was interest, but they were taken aback by the broadcasters who wanted them to fake some of the activity. '**What if nothing happens?**' commissioning editors asked. '**It's going to be a very boring show.**' One major broadcaster was ready to sign it up if they would fake a few special effects, then come clean at the end of the show – as Derren Brown was later to do in a one-off special for Channel 4. But Karl and Yvette stood their ground, insisting that even if nothing happened on the night, it would still be interesting to watch the team dealing with their emotions and the 'scare factor'. The shows where there was no discernible activity would give them a chance to explain to viewers how a paranormal investigation works and what phenomena have to be discounted. Their goal, right from the start, was to conduct a balanced investigation into paranormal activity to try to find out once and for all whether ghosts do exist – and, if they do, what they are.

In October 2001, Richard Woolfe was appointed controller of LIVINGtv, and the first piece of paper he came across in his in-tray was a proposal from a company called Antix Productions for a show that at the time was provisionally titled *Haunting Truths*. He explains: '**I was immediately keen, so I invited Karl and Yvette for a meeting and was impressed by how passionate they were about the project. Then, in a stroke of genius, they handed me a tape with the pilot they had shot. As I sat in the office watching it, I knew we were going to do the show. Yvette is brilliant as the ringmaster, Derek is just amazing and I liked the idea that the entire crew is seen on the show. It was the first series I ever commissioned at LIVINGtv, so it's particularly special for me.**'

He signed them up for an initial series of sixteen shows – and the quest began.

Choosing *Most Haunted* Locations

Around 10,000 locations in the UK have registered, documented hauntings, and there are probably the same again where what's been seen hasn't been recorded, so Yvette and Karl assumed they would be spoiled for choice when deciding where to film. In fact, it was tough getting owners to give permission to film for the first series, because so many felt they had been mocked or misrepresented by previous shows. It was much easier by the second series, when the *Most Haunted* team could demonstrate what they were attempting to do and owners could see it was an honest representation without any gimmicks or punchlines. In fact, by the third series, the team had the opposite problem, with dozens of venues contacting them every week asking to be featured.

They soon became suspicious of owners of commercial premises who could be seeking publicity. Alex Lysaght, the locations manager, explains: **'I get wary if someone contacts me saying they've just opened a nightclub and seemingly there's a ghost on the premises and can we come and investigate as soon as possible … I don't think they realize we're filming up to six months in advance, so we couldn't bump up their Christmas party season for them anyway.'** In fact, a number of places featured in the series have experienced a surge of business after the show airs, but this was never the reason why they were chosen.

The main criteria the team apply when choosing a new location are not visual (whether it will look good on screen) or historical (places associated with famous people or events). Instead, they look for sites that have had a lot of activity within the last few months, where the hauntings have been verified by more than one person – and the more, the better. No matter how many great stories are associated with a castle, priory or stately home, there's no point filming if nothing has been seen in the last couple of years. And if the only sightings are by one slightly peculiar curator or owner, then they're probably not the best bet.

Alex is usually the person who goes on an initial recce to check out locations. **'Ideally we like places where at least three areas are haunted. It won't make such a good show if there's only one room. Also it has to be big enough, because we've got a lot of equipment and a whole team of people to fit in. I get loads of letters from people saying their house is haunted – maybe ten a week – and I've done recces on a couple, but basically most private homes are just not big enough.'**

As she's walking round, Alex has to check practical considerations – little things like whether there's any lighting or electricity, because if not the crew will have to bring a generator. Will there be access for their trucks? Is there an airport nearby that could spoil footage with plane take-off and landing noises?

Alex also considers where they could film on the property and any physical difficulties they might encounter. She smiles to herself when she spots areas that will appeal to the physically intrepid Karl. **'If there's a wall that needs scaling, or any tunnel that needs to be gone through** or a well that you want to go down, I just know that Karl will be straight in there. When the owner points at a decrepit old tower and says "No one's been up there for over 100 years", I always think to myself, "Yep, Karl will be up there for sure."'

Unfortunately, say the team, comfort has never been a consideration when they decide on locations. They've filmed in damp, dark, underground sites, on top of vertiginous towers, in disused, unheated properties in the depths of winter, in lighthouses, prisons, caves, in a morgue – and on some shoots, like Pendle Hill, they don't even have a roof over their heads.

Souter Lighthouse, one of the more unusual locations.

Choosing the Most Haunted Team

If getting the right locations is important, hiring the right team is vital. They have to get on with each other very well indeed when they're going to spend 24 hours together, much of it in the dark and cold, facing something that they don't understand. Yvette explains: '**We can tell in a couple of hours whether someone will fit in or not. They have to be outgoing, with a good sense of humour, but not the type to play practical jokes on camera, because that would risk the show's credibility. They have to be real people, who will cuss and swear on occasion, and they mustn't be vain and just wanting to get on the television. To be an investigator, they have to take it very seriously.'**

Obviously they have to be brave, because it wouldn't make good television if everyone was continually shrieking, panicking and running away. A few crew members have dropped out because they couldn't handle the sheer terror – and there's no sex bias when it comes to fear. One of the big burly riggers, who do the cabling on live shows, dropped out because he couldn't handle it (we'll let him remain nameless). Yvette says: '**They're all cocky when they arrive, yelling "Seen any ghosts yet, love?" and so on, but at 2 a.m., when they have to derig in the pitch black, it's a different matter. I've seen huge guys walking hand in hand across a graveyard in the dark – it was quite sweet really.'** The girls tend to force themselves to confront their fears and even challenge themselves to be braver – but they don't go to the toilet on their own during night shoots. And who can blame them?

Research has shown that you are more likely to get results if the same group of genuine, like-minded people keep working together. The core team of Karl Beattie, Yvette Fielding, Derek Acorah and Stuart Torevell (chief rigger and Yvette's cousin) have been together since the first series. Historian Richard Felix joined them after they filmed at Derby Gaol, which he owns. Jon Dibley (cameraman) and Cath Howe (make-up artist) came on board during the second series and have stuck around ever since, while parapsychologist Dr Ciaran O'Keeffe didn't get involved until the fourth series, along with guest mediums David Wells and Ian Lawman and psychic artist Brian Shepherd.

Richard Felix and Karl at Dudley Castle.

Everyone has arrived through word-of-mouth recommendations, and they've become like family over the years, socializing between shoots as well as learning how to support each other when required. After an especially terrifying night, they'll stay up for a few hours talking it through or go to sleep in the same room. And, as the team has become closer, they've found they work more effectively in situations that require combined energy, like séances, table-tipping or glass-moving.

Of course, they all have to have extremely high professional standards, because conditions on a shoot can be very testing.

Here's Jon Dibley's description of night-vision filming: '**I need to be a maximum of 10 feet away from my subject or it will get blurred, but I can't see anything in the room except through the lens. To the sides, above and below is pitch black. I need to keep the camera as steady as possible or viewers would soon feel seasick watching. The trickiest bit is that I'm quite often walking backwards, so I can film Yvette, Derek or Ciaran coming down a corridor, and I rely on someone to tell me if I'm about to fall down a hole or walk into a wall.**'

Jon Gilbert is responsible for sound recording: '**I don't carry a light source because I've got the mixer, which is fairly heavy, strapped round my neck and I'm holding a boom mic, ready to train it in a different direction if someone says "What was that?" You have to react quickly. I tend to stick close to Ciaran, because he has a laptop and an EMF meter that give off just enough light to stop me tripping over.**'

Stuart Torevell's role is different again: '**I need to light everything in daylight, get some GVs [general views], do Yvette's opening pieces** to camera and the first walk-around. Then, before the lights go out, usually after the crew have had dinner, it all has to be derigged because we can't go tripping over cables in the dark. It's all down to batteries after that. I'm also responsible for health and safety on location, which can be a challenge! And I'm often the one that will tap Jon Dibley on the shoulders to let him know which way to go when he's walking backwards.'

With everyone on such long contracts, it's one of Karl's roles to make sure that complacency doesn't set in – not that there's much chance of that when every single location presents a new, unique set of challenges.

A Range of Belief

The other important factor when putting the team together is that there is a wide range of opinion on paranormal events. It wouldn't make good TV if everyone was jumping up and down, saying '**I believe, I believe!**'

At one end of the spectrum, Derek and the guest mediums have no doubt in their own minds that the spirits of the dead live on and come back to visit us. They see, hear and speak to spirits all the time, and their goal is to convince the rest of us about the afterlife.

Richard Felix believes in ghosts but is sceptical about a lot of sightings. '**I think eight out of ten things can be explained. But before I die, I would like to prove that the dead do return.**'

Stuart Torevell says: '**I've always believed in ghosts from a very early age, and my mind's made up now because I've been through the mill. There are things I've seen, heard and felt that I haven't even told the rest of the crew.**'

Tor O'Neill, the production manager, says: '**I do believe in spirits but I don't believe we're supposed to see them. That's not how it works. I've sensed, felt and heard things but never seen anything.**'

Yvette says she is still sitting on the fence. '**Things happen on shoots that I think must definitely be ghosts, but next morning, in the cold light of day, I start questioning whether there's a rational explanation. It would be lovely to believe that we all go off to heaven and have another life and meet our loved ones again, but then you go back to your normal life and go to the supermarket and do the laundry and you think, "Maybe a breeze did shut that door or ruffle my hair, maybe that wasn't a man's breath in my ear but just a funny sound in the ear itself." I keep questioning all the time.**'

Jon Dibley says he won't believe in ghosts until he has physically seen one with his own eyes, and he is often one of the first to offer a rational explanation for events, but he has felt hot and cold spots and seems quite emotionally susceptible to strong atmospheres.

Cath Howe says there is definitely something but she doesn't know what, and working on the series has made her question it all more than she did before.

Rachel Philips, the script supervisor, says: **'I'm not a 100 per cent believer, but I would like it to be proved one day.'**

Karl believes that 99 per cent of so-called paranormal activity has a scientific explanation. **'I do a lot of discounting, because we're trying to find out if there are ghosts or not. I'm now convinced that there are paranormal happenings, but what are they? The spirits of dead people? An electromagnetic force or a kind of magnetism we don't understand? A particular kind of vibration that causes hallucinations? We've all experienced so many things that we know there's definitely something there.'**

Ciaran O'Keeffe approaches the series as an academic, because he researches parapsychology at Liverpool Hope University. He's witnessed several occurrences he can't find an explanation for and says there's a part of him that thinks, **'Wow! How fantastic it would be to find that evidence!'** But he maintains that he hasn't come across that definitive proof – yet.

Collectively, the *Most Haunted* team aim to put the truth about their experiences in front of viewers and let you make up your own minds. They have varying degrees of belief and scepticism, but all have now seen inexplicable sights, heard noises with no obvious cause, smelled strong scents that come from nowhere and quickly fade again, or experienced powerful emotional swings as they go about their work. Some have been scratched, pushed and physically attacked by unseen forces. And they have all been very, very scared.

Who is Watching?

As soon as the first couple of *Most Haunted* programmes went out, LIVINGtv knew that something unusual was happening. Richard Woolfe explains: '**We were getting a viewing spike when each show aired, and we noticed that people were tuning in at five to nine on Tuesday evenings – I guess they thought we might start early and they didn't want to miss anything. We've since found out that loads of fans have rituals attached to the way they watch the show; they turn off the lights, close the curtains, some burn candles and others set tape recorders running in case there's any EVP** [see p. 115]. **We also discovered that lots of people are getting together to watch the shows, even holding *Most Haunted* parties. From this research, we then decided it would be a great idea to take the programme live as this would give the fans the opportunity to interact with the show.**

'**The first live event was on Hallowe'en 2002 at Dudley Castle, and we knew we had a success on our hands when there were 500 people queuing outside at 7 p.m., two hours before we were due to start. It was a wide range of types – men, women, old, young – very varied, and all of them were prepared to spend three and a half hours sitting in a freezing cold castle courtyard watching the show being filmed.**'

Next came the idea of three-night events. The first one took place over New Year, and the team traced the story of Dick Turpin all the way

Yvette at the first *Most Haunted* live event, at Dudley Castle in 2002.

through Essex to York Racecourse, where he was hanged. '**That was a great New Year**,' says Richard, '**and it includes one of my all-time favourite lines from the show. Derek said he was in touch with a spirit called Mary, and pronounced with great solemnity, "Mary ... loves ... Dick! Mary loves Dick!" Yvette was struggling to keep a straight face. We also had the entire team getting lost in Epping Forest and having to be rescued by a park ranger. And then** [parapyschologist] **Matthew Smith, the sceptic on the crew, was challenged to go out into the middle of York Racecourse, on his own, in driving blizzard conditions. Suddenly we heard him yell through the pitch, pitch black, "Oh my God, I can see lights!" It was a surreal moment, but it turned out to be two people walking their dog in the snow, and holding a lantern.**'

You'll find information about forthcoming live events on the website **www.livingtv.co.uk/mosthaunted** or in flashes after the regular programmes. Karl says: '**It's a great chance for people at home to get**

VIEWING FIGURES

Most Haunted is the most watched paranormal programme in the UK, with regular viewing figures of around 1 million per episode and up to 3 million for live events. In fact, the 2004 Hallowe'en special got higher viewing figures than any programme on terrestrial channels at the time – the first and only time this has happened. The series has been sold in Australia, New Zealand, Canada, the Netherlands, Poland, Ukraine and Israel, and the team have been shooting in the USA during 2005.

Derek with the fans at Dudley Castle.

involved. We had 50,000 calls for tickets for the last live event, and people were queuing for ten to twelve hours, from 9 o'clock in the morning. Yvette and I always go and have a chat, because they're the people who make the show famous. Viewers do see things and strange things do happen. Even if you're at home, safe, you can see potential ghosts through the telly at the same time as we are seeing them.'

He continues: 'We probably get 30 emails a month from people who've just realized they're psychic. There are the ones who still take their dead dogs for a walk and pat them on the head or who think their first hamster is their spirit guide. If they believe it, you can't knock it. As far as I'm concerned, it's a possibility.'

Clare Hollywood, LIVINGtv's commissioning editor, explains how they encourage viewers to get involved: 'The audience seem to like the interactive aspects of the show. If we get calls from 2,000 people at

9.49 p.m. saying they've seen an orb on their TV screen, we'll rewind the tape and have a look, live on air. We get them involved in experiments; if we're searching for a duke, for example, we might ask them to try automatic handwriting [see p. 228] or do a drawing and fax it through to us. People can call, fax, text, email, press the red button or chat on the forums on our website. Over the three-day live events, we get an extraordinary 30 million hits on the website. The audience can choose where the team go by clicking on a map. They can try remote psychometry [see p. 162]. And one audience member at the live events will be selected to go on a vigil. Believe it or not, they try to bribe us in the hope of getting picked!'

After the live events took off, Richard started getting approaches from celebrities who loved the show and wanted to be involved, and so *Celebrity Most Haunted* was born. Then they started making *Most Haunted Extra*, a half-hour show where the team get more of a chance to talk about what happened to them at a specific location and let viewers get to know them a bit better and find out what happens when the cameras stop rolling. There's no doubt that the 'brand' is a huge success.

So does LIVINGtv's Richard Woolfe believe in ghosts himself? He considers the question. 'We've seen a lot of things you can't explain. I'm not saying that the paranormal does or does not exist, but the programme is a legitimate, scientific quest to find out – as well as great entertainment – and I'm very proud of it.'

So, like most of the crew, he appears to be sitting on the fence, still waiting to be convinced!

CHAPTER 2

Baseline Testing

Most viewers probably don't have any idea how much work has been done before the cameras start rolling. Researchers have found out all they can about the location, interviewed eyewitnesses to recent sightings there and trawled through the public records, local libraries and newspaper archives for stories about the property, and they may have done some genealogical research on families associated with the place. Karl will have scripted Yvette's pieces to camera, explaining the history of the building and its hauntings to date, and come up with a basic plan for the 24 hours of the shoot. Alex or Tor will have booked hotel rooms for everyone, arranged to get them all there and made sure that essentials like meals, tea and coffee, chocolate and crisps are on hand. (Tor comments: **'If they don't get nice food, a lovely crew can quickly turn into monsters.'**)

The day before a shoot, the technical side of the team (Karl, Alex, Stuart, Jon Dibley, Ciaran and Jon Gilbert) will go to the location to check it out, do some preliminary filming and help Ciaran to perform what are known as the baseline tests. Some of these require special equipment; the rest just require common sense. Here's what they do.

RESEARCHING YOUR HOUSE

If you think your house is haunted and want to find out about its history, Richard Felix suggests you begin by chatting to your neighbours. 'Ask questions of people who have lived in the area for a long time; you'll get more information from locals than any other source. Then visit your local studies library to find the names of previous owners of the house and search your local newspaper archives (usually on microfiche). Local papers go back to about 1860 and should give you any stories about people who lived in your house, especially if there were crimes, fires or suicides.' There are blank pages at the back of this book for your notes.

Ciaran O'Keeffe making a record of fluctuations in the electromagnetic field.

Karl takes EMF readings in the Edinburgh Vaults.

EMF Readings

An EMF meter is used to measure the electromagnetic field in every room, corridor, attic or cellar where they plan to film and several more besides. There has been a lot of research linking fluctuations in the electromagnetic field with ghost sightings and other kinds of paranormal activity. A medium would tell you that this is because ghosts are an energy force and they disrupt our electromagnetic fields when they come into our atmosphere. Several scientists are working on the theory that EMF fluctuations can cause symptoms like headaches, a feeling of being watched and visual or auditory hallucinations in a certain type of susceptible individual. This is an area that Ciaran himself is researching.

AMERICAN METERS

A lot of ghost investigators in the UK have ordered EMF meters from companies in the USA, without taking into account the fact that America has a different electricity system (110 volts and 60 Hz compared to our 240 volts and 50 Hz). Their EMF meters are gauged to the frequency of their alternating current, so wouldn't pick up anything in a household here.

Whatever you believe, it seems certain that EMF fluctuations affect the experience of those present, so the team need to be aware of them.

A normal EMF reading is between 0.5 and 1.5 milligauss. More than this is unusual, especially if it's fluctuating, and readings above 10 milligauss would be of definite concern. Some paranormal researchers have reported swings of + or − 10, but Ciaran has never verified these claims.

If he finds high or fluctuating readings at a location, the next thing is to look for possible natural causes. Household appliances, such as fridges or microwaves, can affect EMF readings slightly if they are within 2 or 3 feet of the meter. Nearby electric utility cables can also influence the readings, but faulty wiring is the most likely culprit. Ciaran says: **'I've heard several reports of houses where there have supposedly been hauntings but once an electrician had paid a visit, the experiences ceased.'** Thunderstorms might rarely affect EMF readings, but only if the storm was continuous over a couple of hours.

Once Ciaran has established the baseline readings throughout the property, he will keep them on hand for comparison with any readings taken during the night vigil when there seems to be activity.

Temperature

It's important to take the temperature in each of the rooms where the team will be filming and at different points in those rooms. Reports of hot and cold spots just before paranormal activity are commonplace, and mediums say that this is caused by a vortex, a kind of portal through which spirits can travel from another realm. (Some say that 'good' spirits come through hot spots and 'evil' ones through cold spots, but Derek thinks this is nonsense.) From a scientific angle, Ciaran says that falling or rising temperatures can change the physiology of the body and could affect the emotions and the adrenalin 'fear response'.

The team take inside and outside temperatures at every property. Ciaran often uses a weather station with transmitters outside and in to give both readings simultaneously. During the shoot they will use a directional laser thermometer to take readings up to 15 feet away, then compare these with the baseline readings. They also have a thermal-imaging camera (the only one of its kind in the UK) that picks up hot and cold spots; for example, at Bodelwyddan Castle, in north Wales, when they contacted Yvette's grandmother and she felt the spirit holding her hand, the thermal-imaging camera showed everyone else's hands were red while Yvette's was blue!

Weather

Some folk think that dramatic weather conditions, with lots of thunder and lightning, mean more ghost sightings, because they increase the atmospheric energy. At *Most Haunted*, they haven't come to any conclusions, but they check humidity (which could affect the performance of some camera equipment) and atmospheric pressure (which can cause headaches and depression if it's very high or very low). There have been a couple of academic papers investigating a possible connection between air pressure and reports of paranormal activity, but neither found a definite link, so the jury's still out.

Wind could be an important factor if it has a force strong enough to blow open doors and windows or send gusty breezes through cracks. Very windy weather can also make those exposed to it feel 'wired' and 'sensitized', so the team will take it into account. Sudden gusts of wind are a common phenomenon during séances (see p. 54 on the séance at Brannigan's), but wouldn't appear quite so strange if there was a force-10 gale blowing outside.

Moon Phase

Another factor the team have begun to note in recent series is the phase of the moon, because of its documented associations with unusual human behaviour. More violent crimes are committed around the full moon, and patients in mental hospitals become more agitated and require extra medication. Since changes in the gravitational pull of the moon cause tides to turn in the world's largest oceans, it seems probable that they will affect human beings, because our bodies are

The full moon outside the Jamaica Inn.

made predominantly of water (H_2O accounts for 60 per cent of the body weight of the average man). There is no evidence of increased paranormal activity around the full moon, but it might make people more open to suggestion, so it's a factor that the team will note. Did it have anything to do with the remarkably spooky night they spent at Jamaica Inn? (See Chapter 8.)

The Walk-around

Old houses make dozens of different noises for umpteen different reasons. If there's wood in the construction, it will expand and contract as the temperature rises and falls, causing creaks in floorboards and joists.

TESTING SMELLS

In future series, you may see Ciaran using a monitor that detects smells. Since unexplained smells seem to be a common experience for the team, he needs to rule out the possibility of olfactory hallucination, where your memory replays the smell of a past event, and find out if there are actual scent molecules in the atmosphere. It will be tricky, though, as one of the characteristics of paranormal smells is that they fade within a few seconds!

Stepping on a loose floorboard in one room can set off a chain reaction that causes an eerie creaking noise several rooms away. Acoustics can play tricks on the senses, making footsteps on the floor above sound as though they're just behind you. For this reason, the baseline-test team will spread out and walk right round the location in daylight, checking loose floorboards, shouting or radioing to each other when they hear a noise to check what it is. During a shoot, you'll quite often see Ciaran and Karl disappear after some strange noises are heard, to try to locate a natural source, such as one of the crew unloading equipment in another room. (Of course, it's always disappointing when they succeed, as at Kinnity Castle – see p. 118.)

The walk-around stage is very laborious, and viewers may not realize how much time and effort goes into it. All doors are opened and closed and the latches checked to see whether they can swing open on their own or not. If you watch an episode where the crew get a fright because a door opens (or closes) on its own, you should be aware that it has been tested rigorously beforehand and didn't behave in this way, or they wouldn't bother showing you the footage.

Each room and corridor is checked for draughts coming through doors, windows or gaps in floorboards. They check for airlocks in the central heating system and figure out what pipework is nearby, which could echo clanging sounds from the other side of the property. Is there a lot of dust on the floors? Is the ceiling plaster crumbling? Are there insects, bats or rodents around? Everything is noted down on a checklist, ready to be consulted if anything odd happens during the night.

Some places are tricksier than others. Could a loose floorboard have caused that cupboard to fall over at Greengate Brewery? And what on earth could have made a barrel roll down the tracks in the basement? (See Chapter 16.)

The team also check external factors that could affect noise levels in the location. Is there a railway line or busy road nearby? Could geological activity in the area cause slight earth tremors? (This happens more often than you might think in the UK.) Or is there a farm nearby where the cacophony of 4 a.m. milking is going to give the team heart failure on their vigil?

After completing the baseline tests, Ciaran or one of the team will set up trigger objects, lock-off cameras and tape recorders in the most haunted rooms and seal them for an hour or so to see if anything happens (more on this in Chapter 5).

Baseline testing can sometimes raise more questions than it can answer. Before we leave the subject, let's see how the tests worked in one of the most eerie locations the team ever filmed – the notorious Edinburgh Vaults.

Edinburgh Vaults

In 1785, a bridge was built in Edinburgh's Old Town over nineteen large stone arches. The foundations were divided into a set of vaults on either side of the bridge, and soon afterwards these underground vaults became a kind of subterranean city housing those who had nowhere else to go: destitute immigrants from the Scottish Highlands, thieves, pimps, prostitutes, pickpockets and murderers. Burke and Hare, the early-nineteenth-century bodysnatchers, are said to have grabbed many victims here and sold them to medical researchers for up to 12 guineas a body – so long as they were fresh enough. Businesses grew up to serve the seething community: taverns, shops, clothing merchants, providing all the necessities of life underground. There are several tales of crimes committed, like the story of landlady Mary McKinnan, who accidentally stabbed a rowdy customer in her tavern and was executed by hanging.

The Vaults were closed in the early nineteenth century but rediscovered in 1980. Parts have now been opened to tourists, who are led through the dark corridors on guided tours. But they had never been fully investigated by a professionally equipped team.

When the *Most Haunted* crew went in to do their baseline tests a few hours before filming, the first thing they noticed was an EMF reading of around 5 to 6 milligauss – far higher than it should have been. It went down to 2 in some areas (which is still on the high side) then back

Derek, Yvette and Phil Whyman investigate the Edinburgh Vaults.

up again. The curator told them that the only electrical fitting in the Vaults is the lighting system, which shouldn't have affected the EMF readings. The most plausible explanation is that there is a utility cable running in the road overhead, but it is unusual for a cable to cause such high readings on its own. Remember that EMF fluctuations can cause susceptible individuals to experience visual hallucinations or a feeling that they're seeing something out of the corner of the eye or are being watched, and it could certainly account for the feelings of sickness that overcame several people as the night wore on. Derek's explanation for their malaise was that they were picking up the residual energies prevalent throughout the vaults, where so much life and death, violence and evil had occurred.

There are vaults on each side of the bridge. In the Niddry Street South side, the team were aware that there was a road not far overhead,

Yvette felt her arms being grabbed from behind.

so Karl set up his usual method of testing traffic noise. When there is a road near the property, he classifies it as A, B or C, with A being busy and C being dead quiet. He sends someone outside with a walkie-talkie and instructs them to radio the crew inside just before a juggernaut, refuse truck or any large, noisy vehicle comes by. The team inside listens to the noise it makes, perhaps tapes it, and they're then able to compare it with any sounds they hear later in the night and either identify or discount traffic noise as a cause.

The acoustics of the Vaults are quite peculiar, so a lot of time was spent making a noise at one level and checking whether the team below could hear it. That was why they were all so surprised, not long into filming, when they began to hear strange noises whose source they couldn't identify. There were shuffling footsteps, whispers and then banging noises that sounded like heavy furniture being moved around. Could it have been some distortion of traffic sounds that seemed different at night than they had in the daytime? Was it just the acoustics making them appear close by? Tom O'Carroll, the sound engineer, found a pipe that was rattling, which explained some noises but by no means all.

This wouldn't explain why the Blair Street Vaults on the other side of the bridge also had peculiar banging, shuffling and dragging noises – these couldn't have come from the surface, because these vaults are three levels deeper underground and there were no rattling pipes on that side. No one has ever come up with a satisfactory explanation for all the noises in the Vaults, even though Ciaran once spent four days underground doing his own investigation into them. (He took some wonderful photographs of orbs down there – we'll discuss light anomalies in Chapter 7.)

In the Blair Street Vaults, there have been multiple reports of a nasty old man, nicknamed 'Mr Boots', who stalks around pushing visitors, glaring at them and yelling **'Get out!'** Derek quickly picked up on this spirit and described the man to the rest of the crew, but he refused to channel him because he judged him too dangerous.

Meanwhile, many team members began to feel as though they were being pushed. First, Yvette felt her arms being grabbed from behind. (She remarks: **'I always say I want something to happen so we can capture it on camera – but when it does, I can't tell you how scared I am. Words can't describe it.'**) Karl felt a freezing cold hand on his face and then on the back of his neck. Something prodded steadicam operator Craig Harman on the hip. Watching the incidents on tape, you can see people are genuinely responding as though they've felt a real push or touch. There were no physical phenomena in the vaults that could have had this effect, but could their responses be psychological? They were underground, in vaults that everyone described as spooky even when the lights were on. Most (but not all) knew the stories of visitors feeling as though they were being touched or pushed.

Could the high EMF readings have contributed to their jumpiness? Or was there a grounded spirit who wanted them to leave and was doing his utmost to persuade them? What do you think?

CHAPTER 3

How Mediums Work

After the baseline tests have been completed and the set pieces to camera have been filmed, a car is sent to bring Derek to the site. Until the car draws up outside, he has no idea where he is being taken. He has been booked to work on particular days and then, 24 hours before the shoot, Alex will email or phone him with the name and address of the hotel she wants him to turn up at. This hotel could be just 5 minutes' drive from the shoot or as much as 45 minutes' drive away.

For those who suspect that mediums are phonies who do all the research first, just consider how many haunted properties you might find within, say, a 30-mile radius of virtually any hotel in the British Isles. There could be dozens of them, and it would be hard work to become an expert on them all. What's more, Derek is notorious for having a bad memory and can never remember what has happened on shoots he's been on before, never mind recalling dates, names, facts and figures for possible future ones. As Stuart remarked, **'Derek will put down a cup of tea and a minute later forget all about it. That's how bad his memory is!'**

MISTAKEN LOCATION

On psychic artist Brian Shepherd's first shoot with the team, he turned up at the hotel he'd been told to come to and, seeing all the team's vans parked in front, he assumed it was the hotel itself they were investigating. He started doing a walk-around but wasn't picking anything up. Fortunately, Alex put him straight before too long!

Before the mediums are collected, they perform an 'opening up' meditation, in which they ask for protection from whatever spirits await them at the location. Derek has his own, special type of meditation, which he describes as his 'spiritual waterfall'. David Wells performs a procedure using Kabbalistic ritual, asking for protection from archangels and invoking the magical tools of a sword (air), wand (fire), disc (earth) and cup (water). Whatever method a medium uses, the 'opening up' is like sending a signal to your brain to utilize its psychic abilities.

Most mediums don't spend their everyday lives with these abilities 'switched on', or they would end up in a straitjacket before long as all the energies and spirits in the surrounding world crowded inside their head, clamouring to be heard. However, Ian Lawman has found that he can't close down any more. '**It drives me crazy. My fiancée complains that I'm spending more time with the dead than with the living. When I'm walking round the supermarket, I see people's dead relatives alongside them and I want to go up and tell them, but you can't just walk up to strangers with information like that.**'

Ian Lawman listening to spirits.

When Derek arrives at the property, usually about dusk, he will walk around sensing the energies present. As Yvette says, '**This is often when things start kicking off.**' The presence of a psychic medium acts like a magnet for spirits who want to communicate and they begin to come closer to the group to watch what's going on.

There are residual energies, which are like a tape or video recording of past events captured in the fabric of the building. (This theory is known as the 'stone tape' theory.) When someone who is psychically open arrives in a place that has an eventful history, events are replayed in snatches, letting them feel some of the emotions and sensations experienced by past residents. All of us have a certain amount of innate psychic ability, but the more you use it, the more acute it will become.

The mediums' first impressions are likely to be of residual energies, helping them to build a picture of what has gone on in the place previously. For example, when Derek walked into the Edinburgh Vaults, he sensed a crowd of people sitting and making merry, then he smelled ale, and behind the gaiety he could sense anger and negativity. This was at the site of the old tavern where Mary McKinnan had committed a murder.

Next, they will begin to sense the grounded spirits, those who for one reason or another have stayed behind on this earth after they left their physical bodies. Derek explains why this can happen: '**One common reason why spirits do this is fear. If they have performed evil acts in their lifetime, they are afraid to go into the light when they pass over, because they know that they will go to the lowest of the seven realms of God's kingdom and it's not a nice place. It's not hell, as portrayed in Christian religions, but there is a spirit justice for those who have escaped justice on earth.**

'**Another reason why a spirit person may remain grounded is if they have left their body at a young age or committed suicide. The light is not open to them straight away and they're confused; they don't know what to do. Sometimes I help spirits like this after filming has finished for the night. If they are asking to be released, I will help them to find the light.**

'**Some spirits stay grounded because they don't realize they have passed. It may be that they have died very suddenly and unexpectedly in an accident. They're still around their family, rattling objects, making noises, saying "Hey, look at me!", and they can't understand** why they're **not being noticed.**' (This is portrayed by Bruce Willis's character in the popular movie *The Sixth Sense*.)

David explains: '**You still have free will when you leave the physical body, just as you do in life. The light appears but you don't have to go into it. Some spirits choose to stay here because they have scores to settle – for example, if they've been murdered and they want their murderer to be caught. We come across some female spirits who have a grudge against men, and then Yvette will have to communicate with them because they won't come near anyone male.**'

Not all spirits that the mediums see and hear are 'grounded spirits'. More often than not they will be in 'visitation' from the other realms, and they have different ways of making themselves known here. According to mediums, they come into our world through hot and cold spots known as vortexes, which are invisible, tube-like areas about the size of a doorway, just big enough to house a spirit body.

GRAVEYARDS

On the whole, spirits don't want to hang around in graveyards. Once they've left their physical body, they are more likely to visit loved ones at home, so Derek advises you should put your flowers in a vase in the sitting room rather than by a cold, rain-drenched grave. David adds that most spirits will attend their own funeral. They want to see what happens to their physical body – and no doubt they're curious to see who turns up to mourn them!

Spirits can choose where they will visit, so if their loved ones are still alive, they often go to see them. They can return to places they were particularly fond of, that hold pleasant memories for them. And they can travel to several different places (although not at the same time). For example, the spirit of Charles I has been seen at Banqueting House in Whitehall, scene of his execution, but Derek encountered him by the fireplace at Tutbury Castle in Staffordshire, a place he was said to enjoy visiting. Anne Boleyn has been seen at Hever Castle as well as the Tower of London. And Mary Queen of Scots seems to roam between her homes in France and Scotland as well as the different castles where she was held captive in England. Some paranormal investigators think that spirits move along ley lines (more on these on p. 230).

Channelling and Possession

When a medium feels a spirit coming into the atmosphere, they sense their 'essence' – a kind of composite picture of all their life experiences and their personality. Both Derek and David are clairvoyant, clairaudient and clairsentient, meaning that they can see, hear and feel spirit presence (and they can smell it as well). When they feel a spirit approach, they will often get messages through their spirit guides. Derek's spirit guide is, of course, Sam, and David's is a Native American called White Eagle. Spirits who have recently passed over may not have learned how to communicate, or they may not wish to, so the spirit guide will pass on messages and information to the medium.

Derek has often channelled disruptive spirits.

If the spirit wants to communicate directly, it may try to enter the medium's aura in order to use his physical body. Here's how Derek explains the process: **'We are very fortunate in the physical body because we have an auric field that surrounds us, protecting us. No spirit person can penetrate our auric field unless we give them permission. If I say no, the spirit can't jump in. I make my own decisions on this, and follow Sam's advice about whether a spirit is trustworthy or not. However, there are some times when I've misjudged the situation and a crafty spirit that has been grounded for a long time leaps in.'**

(There's a description of this in the next chapter, about Brannigan's Nightclub.)

Even when a malicious spirit with bad intent gets inside, this is not what we know as 'possession'. Mediums can't be possessed as such, because they have the resources to throw out an interloper, but it can drain their energy severely in the meantime. Derek has several safeguards in the people around him, who know what to do in such an event. Either his wife, Gwen, his tour manager, Ray, or, on set, Karl Beattie will take him firmly by the shoulders and repeat '**Derek, come forward**'.

Karl describes it thus: '**Derek has asked me to reassure him and bring him forward in these circumstances. Sometimes I can hear his voice, as if in the distance, saying "I'm coming". A couple of times over the six series we've filmed, I've had to disable Derek because he can become very powerful and occasionally violent when he's taken over.**' As a master of the martial arts Ryu Kyu Kempo and Wadoryu, Karl can bring Derek down safely, without hurting him, by hitting nerve points that disable his legs. Sometimes it's the only option if the spirit he is channelling becomes violent to a crew member. '**It's a health and safety issue,**' Karl explains. '**Derek's a fit guy and it can be very intimidating if he's coming at you, out of control.**'

It is possible for those who are not mediums to become possessed by bad spirits, and Derek believes it's a particular danger for those who mess around with séances and ouija boards without a medium in attendance (more on the team's experiences with these in later chapters). Derek once had to perform a cleansing ceremony on a young woman, very attractive and seemingly with everything going for her, who had been turned into a spitting, swearing wretch by possession. He sat with her every evening for five long weeks before he could get the negative force to leave her, and says he felt drained himself for almost six months afterwards. (Cleansing is not the same as an exorcism – they are only performed by clergy.)

Ian Lawman specializes in 'spiritual rescue work' and since he began work on *Most Haunted*, he has guided many distressed spirits to the light. David does the same. He explains: '**I open a doorway of light and those that want to can leave. At Bodmin Jail, I had just opened a doorway when I felt an influx of spirits – whoosh – going past me. What I didn't realize was that downstairs Richard** [Felix] **had just asked, "Are there any spirits that want to go to the light?" The synchronicity was astonishing.**'

What does it feel like to channel a spirit? Derek describes it like this: '**Once I agree that a spirit can enter, my own spirit self stands to one side. It's as if I'm detached, listening but not hearing clearly the words that are spoken through my physical body. I feel cold, because my spirit is out of its housing. It doesn't feel right, doesn't feel safe, and I can't wait to get back.**'

David says: '**Just before I channel, I feel the spirit put their hands in mine and my whole body tingles. While they're inside, you lose the sensation of your own limbs. Personally, I wouldn't risk it without another medium there in case I need help getting back.**'

Ian says: '**Sometimes you are aware it's about to happen and feel them getting closer, then at other times they power straight into you. Full takeover is like being pushed onto the floor, and your body is numb and cold. You can't get rid of them until they've said what they** wanted to say, then I ask them to leave and let me come forward. On a couple of occasions I've needed help, and Yvette and Karl have both assisted me.'

All three say that it can take several days to recover their energy again after they've channelled a particularly disruptive spirit. They feel tired, lose their appetites and have difficulty sleeping.

DVP and Transfiguration

Some spirits take possession of a medium's voice box once they are inside the auric field, and this is known as direct voice phenomenon (or DVP). *Most Haunted* viewers will have noticed many occasions when Derek's voice deepens, or his tone of voice changes or his vocabulary appears to hail from another era. **'Leave me alone, you varmint,'** he'll snarl, or he will speak as a small scared child, crying **'She hurt me'** (as at Chatham Dockyard).

David had a terrible shock the first time his voice box was taken over, on the *Most Haunted* shoot at Samlesbury Hall in Preston. Here's his story: **'I was with Yvette, Jon Dibley and Richard Felix, and we'd just finished our vigil. There was a naughty spirit who'd been running round the room, occasionally scraping a bit of furniture, and Yvette screamed when she heard it saying "Fuck off" in her ear. I ran towards her and at that moment, the spirit grabbed my throat. I'd never experienced anything like this before because normally I stay in control. I opened my mouth but only strange grunting sounds came out. I gathered my strength and used my Kabbalistic incantations to push the spirit** out, but I was crying convulsively, mainly because of the shock I'd had. After I recovered, I went back into the room and it came at me straight away, grabbing my jaw and forcing my mouth open so that I could only utter odd, distorted squeaks. To get rid of it this time, I had to flood my entire body with light. It was the only time I'd ever had this kind of battle with a spirit and it took me four days before I could sleep properly afterwards.'

As well as using a medium's voice box, spirits can also control their face and posture in a process known as transfiguration. The expression can change to a scowl, sometimes one side of the face will drop or elongate, and you might see the medium spit or hunch or begin to limp, as they take on the characteristics of the spirit in question. Look closely at their face and you can almost see another person looking out of their features.

After filming is over, every medium has their own method of closing down and shutting out the spirit world, so that they can go back to their everyday family lives. Derek explains: 'I let myself go into a slightly meditative state and visualize all the love that is close to me in this earthly life – that of my wife, son, daughter and grandchildren – and that energy is usually enough to bring me down and close out the spirit world.' David says: 'I imagine the chakras in my body closing, like the iris in an eye, then I always say thank you. It's just good Scottish manners!'

Derek, Yvette and Jason Karl do a daylight walkabout at the Drury Lane Theatre, London.

'True' or 'False'?

As Derek and the other mediums walk around a location, they relay the stories they are being told by the spirits and often they are able to give names and dates for the events described. At that stage, Yvette will radio Richard Felix and ask him to check the information in his sheaves of research. When the show is broadcast, a note will appear on screen, either confirming the name and date they've come up with or saying that they have not been able to trace anyone of that name.

It's exciting for all concerned when Derek and David get known facts spot on, as they often do – particularly when it concerns some small detail that it would have been well-nigh impossible for them to divine in any other way. Richard says: '**I am amazed when I've been delving through a local studies library and I come across a document that no one has taken out for decades, then Derek produces that exact information at the shoot. It's uncanny.**' Often the spirits they pick up on have been detected by previous visitors, but if they didn't record their sightings, how could Derek or David have found out about them?

Sometimes the tales Derek relates aren't recorded and so can't be checked or verified. He may spend time relating a sad story of an ordinary person that never made it into official records – perhaps an undiscovered murder, a suicide after a lover left or a tragic accident, like that of the five chambermaids at Aberglasney House, who appear to have died of carbon monoxide poisoning after one of them put something toxic on the fire as they went to bed. All the team can say in those circumstances is that no records exist to confirm the story. Of course, that doesn't mean they're not true.

The spirits Derek and the other mediums communicate with may not be the most famous in residence at that particular property, for the simple reason that the famous ones weren't in visitation that night. Their observations may or may not concur with other sightings. But it's always intriguing for the team when they come out with some details that research proves to be true.

Ciaran O'Keeffe quizzes Derek endlessly: '**What made you say that? What image can you see?**' He's fascinated by the way mediums work and likes to test the processes they use. His PhD focused on paranormal 'claimants' and he is convinced that a minority of psychics genuinely believe they have the ability to communicate with the dead. Ciaran's

SANDBACH OLD HALL

This was one of the occasions when Derek astonished Richard with information he picked up. 'Derek mentioned Scottish soldiers fighting with swords, which is not something I'd come across in my research and it's not in any literature about the Hall. I went away and thought about it. Now, I'm actually president of the Charles Edward Stuart Society and am quite an expert on Bonnie Prince Charlie's march south with his army towards Derby. It turns out that one section of 1,500 Scottish soldiers, under Lord George Murray, took a detour when they got to Manchester to avoid the opposing army. Their detour took them to Sandbach. If even I didn't know that at the time, how could Derek have known?'

view is that some psychics are able to read people quickly and effectively, but, he says, as far as he can make out the process is purely psychological.

Could Derek and the other mediums all be play-acting and faking in a remarkably clever way? The crew are a bunch of honest, forthright individuals who wouldn't be party to fraud. Rachel Philips says: **'I wondered about it before but now I've worked on the show I know for sure that they never set things up. I wouldn't want to be involved if they did.'**

Could the mediums be picking up memories trapped in the fabric of the property, as proponents of the 'stone tape' theory would have you believe? Are they genuinely communicating with the spirits of dead people? Or do they just believe that they are in touch with the dead, but they're not really?

As Karl says, '**There are only three options. They're extremely good actors; they're mad; or they really are in touch with the dead.**'

In the next chapter, we are going to look at one of the rare occasions when Derek got scared by what occurred on a shoot.

CHAPTER 4

Brannigan's Nightclub, Manchester

Up and down the length and across the breadth of the British Isles, old churches and chapels have been sold to developers and converted into bars, nightclubs and restaurants. If, as some people believe, the spirits of the dead can return to earth, and often come to visit places that were important to them and to air grievances, could church conversions provoke religious types who disapprove of the new role of their previous place of worship?

When the Albert Hall was completed in Manchester in 1910, it was a dream come true for the Reverend Samuel Collier, giving him a base for his Manchester and Salford Methodist Mission. He attracted the largest Methodist congregation in the world at the time to hear him preach about the evils of drink, fornication, vanity and 'dancing to the devil's music'. Ironically, that same hall is now home to Brannigan's, one of Manchester's most popular nightclubs, and it seems that someone – or something – disapproves.

Could it be the Reverend Collier who keeps smashing glasses, tipping liquor bottles off shelves, switching the lights on and off, and pushing visitors and staff around? Suzanne Vinton, *Most Haunted*'s script

Yvette by the great church organ that Karl nearly fell down inside.

supervisor, and Cath Howe, their make-up artist, live locally and had visited Brannigan's before the shoot. Friends of theirs had actually seen a glass levitating a few inches off the bar before being smashed to the ground; in fact, several people have witnessed this over the years. And they knew better than to go to the toilets, where a ghost is said to reach out and touch you while you use the facilities! Staff members have been pushed down the stairs, and they report taps turning themselves on full blast when no one is nearby.

The team knew it was likely to be an eventful night, with so many reports of recent activity, but they had no idea quite how terrifying it would turn out to be.

The nightclub takes up the ground floor of the building, but the old chapel still stands above it, eerie and deserted. Paranormal investigator Phil Whyman took the EMF readings (which were normal) and used a laser thermometer to take temperatures throughout the building (which were warm – 16 to 17°C). He positioned motion detectors on either side of the staircase where staff were often pushed, and he placed glasses round the edge of the balcony to see if a spirit tried to knock them off.

Soon after Derek arrived, he identified four active spirits there – three good, benevolent men of the cloth, who were acting as guardians to contain a dark, angry spirit, that of Godfrey Parks, a murderer who had never been caught.

They got early warning of the kind of violence Parks was capable of when Derek and Karl decided to climb a vertical ladder inside the huge church organ. Karl explains what happened: **'I felt a cold draught, my nose started to run, my chest felt tight, then something pushed me and almost put me through that small hole that we were climbing**

SPIRIT LEVELS

Spirits can exist on different levels. At Brannigan's, Derek described two children, Elizabeth and Philip, running around and playing with each other. Godfrey Parks sometimes tries to chase them but he can't catch them because they are on a different spirit level. Other psychics who have visited Brannigan's have also picked up the names Elizabeth, Philip and Godfrey there.

up through … **Straight after that, my legs just refused to hold me …**
It's the first time I've actually felt a proper thud like that.' As regular
viewers will know, Karl is one of the most pragmatic members of the
team, but he has no doubt whatsoever that he was pushed on that
ladder. And this was just a foretaste of the danger the whole team
would confront as the night wore on.

The Tower

Several crew members heard a loud bang coming from the direction of
the old tower and they decided to go up there to see what was going
on. It was accessible only by climbing a steep ladder and, knowing what
had happened to Karl earlier, everyone felt very apprehensive as they
climbed upwards, especially when Derek heard a spirit shouting **'Don't**
you dare come up here!' Cath said her legs were like jelly.

At the top, Yvette noticed a very strong smell of baby sick, which
was verified by Phil and Derek before it faded away. (See p. 115 for
more about the noises they captured on dictaphone in the same place,
which many thought sounded like a baby crying.)

Shortly afterwards, Derek began holding his nose, complaining that
someone was messing with it, and then the spirit of Godfrey Parks
appeared to enter him. His voice, posture and manner changed abruptly
and he stormed angrily around the tower, strutting up to crew members
in a threatening way. Yvette instinctively hid behind Phil.

'This belongs to me. No one else. Me!' he boomed. He charged up
to Phil Whyman (**'I thought I was going to get hit,'** Phil recalls), then
stared down the lens of the camera yelling **'And you!'** in an aggressive

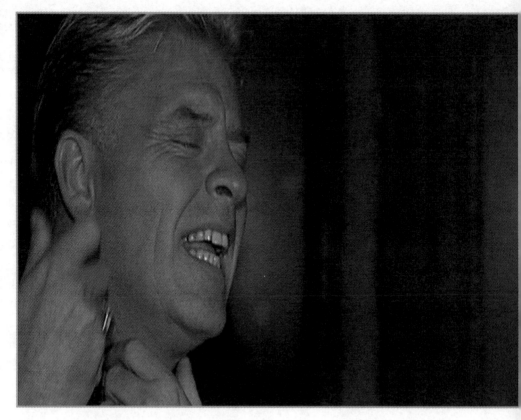

Derek is taken over by Godfrey Parks.

voice, quite different from his own. Craig Harman was filming on a narrow raised ledge when suddenly Derek ran at him and leapt up with no concern for his personal safety, without even looking to see where he was putting his feet. The entire crew were terrified.

Here's Derek's recollection of events: '**I'd never come across what Godfrey Parks did to me that night. I didn't realize what his intent was, but he cajoled me to go into another room on a higher level, and there another spirit jumped inside me. There were two of them, a cohort, and they gave me the feeling that they'd crippled me, that I'd lost the use of my legs. Their strength took me completely by surprise.**'

Yvette asked, '**What do we do? Will he just come out of this himself?**'

Karl realized it had gone too far. Derek was oblivious to everything around him and didn't appear to recognize anyone there. He laughed maniacally as they began trying to talk him down, reassuring him and saying '**Derek Acorah, come forward**'.

'**Get you away ... Hallelujah ... I will push and I will damage you,**' the spirits cried, until, at last, Derek managed to evict them and collapsed in a heap on the floor without any feeling in his legs. '**Get me out, please,**' he begged, and the voice was Derek's own again. His legs wouldn't work so Karl had to carry him down the steep ladder to the floor below.

Karl revives Derek after his ordeal.

It took four days for Derek to recover physically from his ordeal. He had big white patches on his thighs, couldn't eat or sleep, and seemed so ill that his wife Gwen wanted to take him to hospital. It took him even longer to recover mentally and emotionally. '**It made me question Sam and other souls about the true abilities of evil spirits like Godfrey Parks … One minute I was in control and the next minute gone. He wanted to take me into an abyss … And I have to consider whether I am likely to confront such evil again, and how I would cope next time … I don't mind admitting that, for the first time, I was scared. Very scared.**'

The Séance

You'd think that Derek's experience would have been enough for the team, but their mission is to spend 24 hours in each location, investigating as fully as they can. With so many active spirits roaming on different levels at Brannigan's, they felt it might be a good idea to hold a séance and see who came forward, so the entire crew sat down in a circle in the old chapel and joined hands.

Straight away odd things began to happen. Yvette felt freezing cold. Some of them thought they could sense movement in one corner of the hall. They all heard what sounded like mocking laughter, and Richard Felix was prodded in the back. He says: '**It was the first time that had ever happened to me like that.**' Then there were tiny footsteps and Cath Howe felt something touching her shoulder. Tor O'Neill remembers: '**I heard laughing and footsteps that sounded as though someone was scuttling towards us.**' Yvette thinks it was like a child's footsteps running round them – perhaps one of the children who used to attend Sunday school there? Then, she says, '**Suddenly an almighty wind blew through that top floor. We'd been there a long time and hadn't felt so much as a draught before. There were no doors or windows open, and it wasn't even a windy night. It was a real howling sound, like a scene in a horror movie, and it was very frightening.**'

So much happened at Brannigan's that all of the crew who were there remember it as one of the scariest of their *Most Haunted* experiences. Everyone felt or heard something during the séance. Cath says: '**I had**

During the séance, many heard what they thought were children's footsteps.

nightmares for weeks afterwards because I just didn't know what had happened to Derek, and because of the children we'd heard. The whole night, there seemed to be a lot of commotion. Someone definitely didn't want us to be there.'

Derek doesn't believe anyone should try to hold a séance without an experienced medium present or a spirit could target the most sensitive person in the group and try to get inside them. A medium acts as a kind of spiritual lightning conductor, protecting everyone else in the circle. The more mediums you use, the more energy there will be and the more likelihood that spirits will be attracted to your circle.

The way the *Most Haunted* team do séances is usually to sit in a circle, holding hands and visualizing the energy flowing through their left arms and across their bodies to the right and in to the next person. They place their feet on the floor with legs uncrossed. They dim the lights and close their eyes as well.

Yvette explains: 'I talk to the spirits sincerely, as if I'm talking to someone who's still alive. I keep asking them questions, or ask them to give me a sign that they're there.' Karl says: 'I've heard lots of people make the mistake of saying "Is anyone there? Knock once for yes and twice for no." It always makes us laugh.' (Think about it.)

In a *Most Haunted* séance, everyone in the circle takes a turn to do the talking. They say that some of the most common signs of a spirit presence are unusual smells that are intense but fade within a few seconds, hot and cold spots, or knocking sounds. It can help if they place an object or picture associated with the person they're trying to contact in the middle of the circle. Alternatively, they have a lit candle in the centre and ask the spirit to blow it out. Yvette recalls: 'We did this at

Leap Castle, in Ireland. We didn't notice at the time because we had our eyes closed, but the flame bent right over to the side just after we asked if a spirit would blow it out. We only noticed it when we watched the tape later.'

'If there is a disturbance, or anyone feels unwell or passes out, we tell the spirits to go away,' Yvette says. 'I speak firmly and order them to leave. Some say you shouldn't break the circle for any reason, but I think you have to if one member of the group is in trouble.'

Séances can be useful and provide some very interesting results, but they are not a game. In the worst-case scenario, people have gone mad after taking part in a séance, although they may have been disturbed beforehand. The *Most Haunted* team usually try a séance towards the end of a vigil if they feel they want to clarify some earlier spirit experiences or try one last time to make contact in that place. However, they are split down the middle on the subject of ouija boards (see Chapter 8) and have developed some alternative methods they prefer. (These are discussed in Chapter 13.)

CHAPTER 5

Moving Objects

At every single location they investigate, the *Most Haunted* team set up a trigger object in a sealed room. They choose a room that is reported to have a lot of activity and then select an object that would have significance for the spirit that is supposed to haunt there – a personal possession, for example. If it's the spirit of a child, they might leave a toy. In a prison, where people were often waiting to die, or somewhere with an ecclesiastical history, they will leave a cross.

DATING SPIRITS

Karl suggests that one way of finding out what era a spirit comes from is to leave coins from several different periods. You can buy these relatively cheaply from coin collectors. If the coin that moves is a Victorian farthing, you may have a Victorian ghost. If it's an Edwardian shilling, you may have an Edwardian ghost. The theory is that they're most likely to touch the coin they recognize.

It won't be mentioned in the programme that airs if nothing moves, but they try the experiment at every site, usually just after the baseline tests and before filming has begun.

In earlier series, the trigger object was placed on a piece of paper and an outline was drawn round it neatly in pencil. Later, they began to lay the object on a background of sprinkled flour, to rule out the possibility of a rodent nudging it (which would leave footprints in the flour) or a strong draught blowing it (which would displace the flour). A lock-off camera (fixed in position, without anyone operating it) is set up pointing directly at the object, and a dictaphone or MP3 recorder is left to record any sounds. Sometimes they use a motion detector with a laser beam about 3 feet off the ground, to ensure that no one can tamper with the trigger object without setting off an alarm. The door to the room is then locked and sealed with tape.

If you want to try a trigger-object experiment at home, leave the object for as long as you like – 24 hours or more – although you'll have to make sure your film doesn't run out. You can buy motion detectors and surveillance cameras that are triggered by movement at DIY stores and voice-activated tape recorders at electrical-goods shops. If you choose them, you won't waste tape or film while nothing's going on.

Ciaran usually only leaves the trigger object for an hour. First of all, this is because the team need access to the room once Derek begins his walkabout. Secondly, as Ciaran points out, if you taped for 24 hours, you would then have to watch and listen to 24 hours of playback – and if there's more than one trigger object, you would have a lot of very boring viewing.

WHY FILM IN THE DARK?

No, it's not so that they get that spooky effect with pupils looking huge and white and the background having a ghostly greenish tinge. The theory is that spirits find it easier to come into our atmosphere when it is dark because it slows down their vibrations. The *Most Haunted* team use infrared (zero lux) cameras that can capture images in total darkness. Sometimes a team member might use a torch just to see where they're going, but most of the time the only available light is the dim glow of the infrared.

Except … there are a couple of tricks you can use if you have professional equipment. Using Avid editing facilities, an editor can superimpose the first and last frames of the footage and see whether there has been any movement. If there has, they will then have to watch the whole thing to find out what happened. With sound, you can play the first 15 to 20 minutes of a tape and take the levels of ambient sound, then set your monitor to detect anything above that level in the rest of the tape. These are shortcuts – but to be thorough, you really have to watch and listen to the whole thing. And as the *Most Haunted* team usually have 18 cameras running for up to 24 hours each at any given location, that can take a while.

In this chapter, there are descriptions of some moving objects that the team have – or haven't – caught on camera. **'The ones you don't get on film drive you crazy,'** says Yvette. **'At the Galleries of**

Justice in Nottingham, a cross moved but we didn't have a camera on it. You could kick yourself. But we can't be everywhere at once, unfortunately.'

Derby Gaol

The trigger object chosen at Derby Gaol was a cross, because the site used to have links with a nunnery. The cross was placed on a sheet of white paper and an outline drawn round it, then the room was sealed off with tape. When they went back to check, everyone was astonished to find that the cross had moved a good 7 or 8 mm outside the outline. **'What do you bet that the tape ran out and we haven't caught that on camera,'** Yvette predicted – but she was wrong. When they played back the tape, it showed the moment when the cross moved quite clearly. First of all, the paper ripples slightly beneath it; the ripple moves towards the cross, then shifts it with an obvious thrusting movement. Karl says: **'We tried to reproduce that rippling effect afterwards, using the same paper and cross, and while we could pull the paper and get it to move, we couldn't make it bubble and ripple like that.'**

There's nothing in the frame that could possibly have caused the movement, but in retrospect the team wish they had set the camera angle wider to show the area around each side more clearly. Still, it's an incredible piece of footage. If you haven't seen it yet, be sure to get hold of a copy!

Chillingham Castle, Northumberland

It wasn't a trigger object that moved here but a box, in the dungeon while Karl was down there on his own. '**I do tend to go off on my own, for whatever reason,**' he explains. '**A lot of this is a personal thing. Anyway, I'm down in this torture chamber, below the ground, and walking very carefully because there's a lot of stuff on the floor. I could hear noises, like rapping on glass, and I was getting pretty spooked. All of a sudden, I heard something moving very close to me**

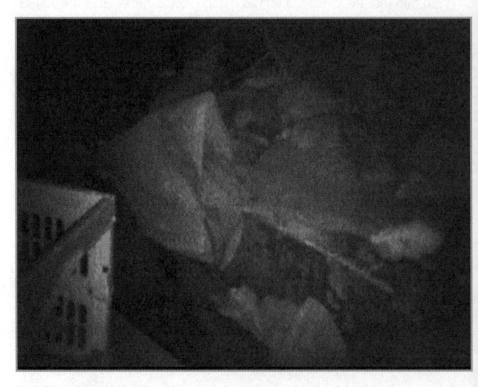

The white laundry basket that moved on camera in the dungeon at Chillingham Castle.

and I turned and ran out. **What you don't see on camera is that I ran straight into this piece of torture equipment!**'

Later examination of the film showed something very curious. There's a white plastic basket, similar to the type people use to put laundry in, sitting on a table. As Karl creeps around, listening to the unfamiliar sounds and getting spooked by the atmosphere, the box moves very distinctly on the table. Karl hadn't focused the camera directly on it, but you can see it finishes at a different angle than it started out at. '**It was a very strange place,**' he says, '**very oppressive.**'

When Derek was brought down to the dungeon later, he walked straight over to the box and said he could detect a vortex there. According to him, '**When things move, it can be energy that comes through a portal and is interested in what we're doing, or a grounded spirit trying to draw our attention.**' What could it have been in the dungeon at Chillingham Castle? Why did a laundry basket move all by itself?

Athelhampton Hall, Dorset

Derek was drawn towards an upstairs bedroom by the spirit of one of the Martyn sisters, great-great-granddaughters of the man who built the hall in 1485. He described how this sister, the 'Grey Lady', would walk the halls and passageways of this fine manor house. Suddenly, the team froze as they heard a rhythmic creaking sound from the next room. When they went through, they found a centuries-old baby's crib rocking backwards and forwards, although no one had been near it.

There were no other entrances to the room apart from the one to the corridor, which was in full view of the team.

Later that night, Yvette and paranormal investigator Jason Karl sat in the dark watching that crib, hoping against hope that it would move again on camera. Unfortunately, it was not to be – but they did see some remarkable sparkly lights moving around the crib, getting brighter, as though a spirit was standing watching over a child. (There's more about light anomalies in Chapter 7.)

Spirit lights flickered around the crib at Athelhampton Hall.

Drury Lane Theatre, London

The oldest surviving theatre in London, built in 1812, Drury Lane is said to have at least five ghosts, but the one most frequently seen is the 'Grey Man' who watches the stage from the circle balcony or from seat number D1 in the stalls. In 1939, the 70-strong cast of a show called *The Dancing Years* was assembled on stage for a group photograph when most of them saw the Grey Man, wearing eighteenth-century clothing, standing up in the circle. Derek identified him as Arnold Woodruffe, an actor who had been murdered and whose remains had been bricked up behind a wall backstage. '**I will never forgive him. Jealous of my talent … How dare he?**' he thundered, when Derek channelled his spirit.

Stuart Torevell and cameraman Rick Fielding (Yvette's brother) turned their attention to seat D1. They sat in it for a while, in the dark, and noticed a strange light nearby. As he stood up, Stuart was filmed clearly putting the seat back into its upright position. Minutes later, they turned and saw that the seat had spookily come down again on its own. They checked the hinges and springs but the seat was designed and balanced to rest upright and needed some pressure applied to bring it back down again. Who – or what – had applied that pressure? The team could find no explanation. (There's more about Drury Lane Theatre in Chapter 7.)

Maes Artro, Gwynedd

There are many different buildings on this 10-acre site, which used to be an RAF base during the Second World War. Ciaran decided to set up a trigger object in the museum, where wartime memorabilia is housed: old uniforms and medals as well as the relics of plane crashes. According to staff, a poltergeist regularly interferes with the exhibits, and they often find them moved or knocked over when they open up in the morning. Ciaran set up an MP3 recorder, a camera primed to take Polaroids at regular intervals and five 1940s coins arranged in exact positions on a sheet of squared paper on a bed. The room was then padlocked and left under guard.

When they returned, the first thing they noticed was that there were puddles of water on the floor. There was a violent storm with gale-force winds raging outside – '**Classic haunted house weather,**' quipped Yvette – but they couldn't find any leaks in the ceiling or walls of the museum. Producing puddles of water is a fairly common poltergeist trick, but Ciaran decided that some kind of undetected leak was more likely.

Next they noticed that a torch left on at the bedside in the museum had gone out at some point during the night. But what astonished them most of all was that the coins had all shifted slightly across the paper. Derek was called in and he identified the poltergeist as Flight Lieutenant Geoffrey Paige. Derek asked him to show himself and they all heard a strange, wheezy kind of laugh – '**hah, hah, hah, hah, hah**' – that was picked up on tape as well.

Was there a rational explanation for the disturbances in the old RAF museum? Or had the resident poltergeist been busy? (For more on the extraordinary three days the *Most Haunted* team spent at Maes Artro, see Chapter 13.)

The Station Hotel, Dudley

Room 214 was said to be the site of much activity in this spiritually lively hotel in the West Midlands, so the team focused their attention there. After an eventful vigil by the girls, they set up a lock-off camera at 3.30 a.m. and sealed the room for an hour. When looking back at the tapes later, Karl superimposed the first and last frames and realized that at some point the bed and chair had moved by around a foot. He looked back through the footage at normal speed and couldn't see any obvious movement. It was only when it was speeded up 30 times that you could see the bed and chair shifting sideways for no apparent reason. Could it be caused by the ghost of the lady in white that several people claim to have seen sitting in that chair, watching over them as they slept?

From the technical corner, Ciaran says: '**To be strictly scientific, we should have had a structural engineer assess the stability of the building, find out whether it was affected by movements of trains or traffic nearby and if the floor is perfectly level.**' But there was so much more activity during the 24 hours at the Station Hotel that train vibrations couldn't begin to account for all of it. There's a fuller description in the next chapter.

Derek and the cupboard that nearly toppled over at Greengate Brewery.

The team have witnessed many more moving objects over the series they've filmed: a teddy bear at Mary King's Close in Edinburgh (see p. 141); some flying books at Owlpen Manor (see Chapter 14); and a rolling beer barrel in Greengate Brewery (see p. 218), as well as stones being thrown, a cupboard almost toppling over, doors closing, curtains moving and many other heart-stopping moments. We'll cover as many of them as we can in later chapters.

CHAPTER 6

The Station Hotel, Dudley

Some paranormal experts categorize poltergeist activity into five different levels:

- **Level 1** involves the senses – people hear strange sounds, experience hot and cold spots and feel as though they're being watched.

- At **level 2** there are unusual smells, loud noises and sudden breezes blowing across the area for no obvious reason.

- **Level 3** is physical – appliances or light switches are turned on and off or doors open and close when there is no human being nearby.

- At **level 4**, objects move, they disappear from one place and turn up in another or they are thrown.

- **Level 5** can be dangerous. People are slapped, bitten, scratched, punched, pushed around or even thrown across a room.

The word 'poltergeist' comes from the German words '*poltern*' (meaning knocking or noisy) and '*geist*' (ghost). In many reported cases of poltergeist activity, a pre-pubescent child or adolescent is particularly targeted. Derek believes that their sensitivity makes it easier to create a vortex around them. He explains: '**It's not straightforward for spirits to learn how to move objects and so forth. When they pass over to other realms, they are like children again and face a learning curve before they can affect anything back on earth.**' This is amusingly visualized in the film *Ghost*, when Patrick Swayze's character is in the subway and sees another ghost throwing a punch. He hadn't realized it was physically possible to make contact in this way because when he had tried, his arm had gone straight through objects, but after a bit of practice, he got the hang of it. According to Derek, '**A spirit person would have to try many, many times to hone a particular skill – it could take them years in our time – but once they've learned, there's no stopping them.**'

There appears to be more than one active spirit at the Station Hotel in Dudley but, from what the team observed, between them they have mastered all five levels of poltergeist activity.

Richard Felix had unearthed some grisly stories attached to this pleasant and normal-seeming hotel. A chambermaid had been murdered by the hotel manager and hidden in a beer barrel in the cellar in the early 1900s. A boxer called Tipton Slasher had reportedly hanged himself in the cellar after visiting a medium called Theophilus Dunn, who told him that he would lose his next fight and all his money into the bargain.

Guests and staff alike had been reporting uncanny events all over the hotel. In the cellar, beer barrels appeared to be able to move by themselves. In the restaurant, a ghostly man in black they nickname 'George' is often seen sitting at a particular table, and knives have been hurled through the air towards unwitting staff. Guests who stay

ELECTRICAL APPLIANCES

The *Most Haunted* team have experienced several examples of electrical equipment switching on and off when no one was nearby. In Derby Gaol, a cardboard box had been left on top of a cooker that was switched off but they suddenly began to smell burning. The cooker had come on by itself and then, to add to the confusion, the fire alarm went off. At Souter Lighthouse in Tyne and Wear, an industrial dishwashing machine in the kitchen came on suddenly.

But the spookiest incident of all was at the Manor House Restaurant in West Bromwich. Stuart, Karl and Rick Fielding were in a bedroom when there was a loud bang and the television came on by itself. Karl quickly directed a camera to show that the remote control was on top of the set and hadn't been triggered by any of them. It was only later that he realized the TV hadn't even been plugged in at the wall. Karl says: 'It was probably the scariest thing that had happened at that point. I never found out what caused that big bang, although I checked everything. And there's no natural way a TV could come on when it's not plugged in. TVs can't store power, because they don't have generators.' The team have no explanation for any of these occurrences.

Richard in the cellar of the Station Hotel, where a chambermaid may have been murdered.

in rooms 213 to 217 (particularly 214 and 217) have often rushed, terrified, down to reception in the middle of the night, asking to be moved to another room and claiming 'something' was in the room with them. Many have reported seeing a lady in white sitting in a chair or walking through the wall. On top of this, there have been cold spots, dark shadows, whispers, papers moved from desks and people claiming they have been touched when there's no one nearby. Who could be responsible for all this activity?

The team's bizarre experiences in the Station Hotel began the night before shooting was due to start:

- Phil Whyman had been allocated room 214 to sleep in, and he came to breakfast the next morning insisting that his bed had moved in the middle of the night.

- As Craig Harman was setting up a camera in the restaurant, a knife suddenly clattered to the ground at his feet, although there was nobody who could possibly have thrown it. And seconds later, something tugged the edge of his T-shirt.

When Derek arrived at the hotel, as usual having had no idea where he was being taken, he asked straight away to go down to the cellar. There he quickly picked up that there had been a murder and he identified the victim as Elizabeth Ann Hitchin, a girl who worked there. She had been having an affair with the manager, whom Derek named as '**George**', and was threatening to tell his loved ones so he strangled and then stabbed her. Derek described her body being dragged by the legs and then pulled up through the chute the barrels are delivered down. He believes that her body is buried in the grounds not far from the entrance to the chute and that she is the '**woman in white**' who haunts the hotel bedrooms she used to clean and tidy.

Richard and Phil; the EMF readings were fluctuating in the cellar.

Locations manager Suzanne Vinton in room 214.

In the restaurant, Derek identified the 'man in black' as George Lawley, an expert in ale, and said he knew about the murder, although he was not the murderer. Richard quickly located a man of this name in historical records and told them that he was a brewer's traveller, who lived from 1845 to 1935 and wrote a book on the history of the area.

It was with more trepidation than usual that the team split into separate groups to spend their vigils in the dark. Yvette, Cath Howe and Suzanne Vinton went to room 214, where they hoped the chambermaid might be more likely to appear to a group of women. Sure enough, things soon began to happen. All three of them saw some very clear, sparkly lights floating just beside the chair.

'The lights were a kind of mist,' Cath recalls. 'Yvette asked the spirit to show us again and it did. You can explain a lot of things, but it's hard to explain that.'

Soon after, Yvette began to feel her thighs burning up with an intense heat that the others could detect through her trousers. At the same time, Cath was feeling as though her cheeks were hot, even though the room was a bit on the chilly side. Seconds later, she jumped as she felt the bed move. They all felt it, and got very, very scared – but it was only the next morning that the team noticed three very distinct scratch marks on Cath's left cheek. Could she have accidentally caused them herself? Her nails are neat and well manicured, as a make-up artist's have to be. She doesn't remember feeling the scratches happen – just the sensation of her face being hot.

Yvette felt a strong sensation of heat in her thighs.

PSYCHOKINESIS

Known to those in the trade as PK, this is a much-disputed phenomenon. Can human beings concentrate their minds to cause objects to move? Or could some kind of paranormal force influence the subconscious brain to produce certain effects? Ciaran says: 'There has been some very impressive research at Princeton University, where subjects were able to affect the decay of radioactive material just by using the power of their minds, but I haven't seen any convincing evidence of objects being moved by PK.' Karl says: 'I personally think it's something we have the ability to do ourselves, up to a point. I think it's a mass energy we can build up. It's a scientific fact that energy never disappears - it just dissipates. If people can produce this mass energy when they're alive, the ability is still there when they're dead.'

Meanwhile, down in the cellar, Phil was picking up some EMF fluctuations near the floor, although the readings had been normal when he checked the area earlier. Karl was complaining of a terrible headache, as if his skull was being crushed in a vice – a symptom he's experienced a few times when there are EMF fluctuations. Then they all saw a clear spirit light, and moments later Derek said the spirit had left. Simultaneously Karl's headache disappeared. It was after all this that a lock-off camera captured the bed and chair moving in room 214.

Ciaran is particularly fascinated by the light anomalies at the Station Hotel, since they were seen by all present as well as caught on camera. Is chambermaid Elizabeth Ann Hitchin still patrolling the rooms she used to take care of a century ago? Is George Lawley still hanging out in the restaurant he used to supply in the days when he was a brewer's traveller? Is the murderer still haunting the scene of his crime? Or could there be natural explanations for all the poltergeist activity at the Station Hotel? You decide.

What Do Ghosts Look Like?

What do ghosts look like? How would you know if you had seen one? Very few of us can claim to have seen a spirit figure standing straight in front of us as clearly defined as a living person. Most reported sightings are shadowy, out of the corner of the eye, and so indistinct that moments later you begin to question what you saw. If spirits want to communicate with us, why don't they appear clearly and definitely, so there could be no doubt about it?

This is Derek's explanation: '**The spirit realm is of a faster vibration than ours, so if they showed themselves on a visitation we'd be blinded; they are too bright and too fast … Imagine a private plane, say an eight-seater Piper with external propellers. You can walk over to that plane and touch the propeller and it feels cold, like normal metal. You can see it and, if you lean in close, you may be able to smell the metal, but one thing is missing, because it's stationary. Once the pilot turns the engine on, the momentum builds up until the propeller is just a fuzz. If you didn't know anything about planes, you would say there's no propeller there, just a vague fuzzy impression. This is like spirits. They are coming so fast that your eyes are not trained enough** to see, unless the captain turns the engine off. Mediums have trained themselves to turn the speed down and that's why they can see more clearly than those who are not mediums.'

David Wells uses a different metaphor: '**Ghosts operate in a different vibration. It's similar to why we don't see television pictures as they zap through the air into our TVs.**'

According to Derek, when spirits pass over they have to learn how the spirit world works. At first, the most they can manage to show us is some sparkly lights or orbs, a primitive manifestation of their energy, which can be captured by digital cameras and sometimes seen by the human eye as well. As the spirit becomes more experienced, or the viewer becomes more psychically open, there will be a coming together so that you can see an outline or a fuzzy shape – but not all such shapes are spirits in visitation. The traditional description of a ghostly white shape floating across the floor is more likely to be residual energy than a spirit person returning, Derek says.

Mediums learn to see spirits so clearly that they can make out their features, details of clothing and nuances of expression. Derek is convinced that the *Most Haunted* cameras will capture a full manifestation one day if the same close team keep working together. '**Spirits need energy to stay in our atmosphere and they can gather this energy most effectively from a séance or table-tipping session made up of open, like-minded people. The more the team work together, and the more psychically open they become, the more likely it is that a spirit will be able to appear to them.**' Keep watching so you don't miss it!

ECTOPLASM

Derek claims that he is progressing towards the stage when he will reach 'physical mediumship' and be able to produce ectoplasm. This is a substance that develops naturally in the physical body that a very few mediums (only two in the world at present) can produce through their nostrils, mouth and ears and allow a spirit person to energize in it. When this happens, he says, he will demonstrate his skill all over the world, and those who attend his demonstrations will be able to see their loved ones housed in the ectoplasm. Some mediums even allow you to come forward and embrace it. Needless to say, Ciaran is very sceptical about ectoplasm.

Spirit Lights

Viewers who have followed *Most Haunted* from the first series through to the sixth will realize that the team are much more likely to discount light anomalies in later episodes. Experience has taught them that there can be umpteen reasons why flickering lights appear on film – but that means that when they draw your attention to peculiar light effects now, it's because they can't find any natural explanation for them.

Ciaran thinks that most light anomalies seen on camera can be accounted for by dust particles. If they are spotted at the time rather than back in the studio, he might try to test for this by using a pipette to blow air in front of the camera to see if it produces the same kind of effect. You can always check the amount of dust in the atmosphere by holding up a torch and blowing into its beam.

Another possible cause of light anomalies can be an insect flying in front of the lens. Different insects have individual flight patterns, but you can usually pick out the floaty meanderings of a moth or the busy zigzags of a house fly or a wasp.

Karl says that they discount a lot of light anomalies in the editing suite. '**When it comes to camera reflection, we know what to look for now. It's the same with faults on the film. What's odd is when you see the lights following something physical or when you see them with the naked eye rather than through a lens.**'

Ciaran has contacts in the photographic world who help him to analyse photographs with light anomalies. '**These guys are so specialist that they can look at a picture and say, for example, "That was taken with a digital camera, probably a Sanyo, and the autofocus function was switched on." They're very specific.**'

The problem is that orbs usually only show up on digital cameras, as opposed to Polaroid or regular ones. A recent three-year investigation showed that some kinds of digital camera are better at capturing them than others. Ciaran gets sent a lot of movies with pulsating orbs and he can explain them straight away, because that's exactly what happens when you get dust in front of a digital camcorder that's switched to autofocus. '**The camera can't decide whether to focus on a dust particle or the object behind, so it "pulses" between the two.**' It's more impressive when orb photos are taken with manual focus.

Ciaran's pictures of light anomalies in the Edinburgh Vaults were taken with a Polaroid camera, and he has worked hard with colleagues at Kodak to try and reproduce the effects. **'We tried with a thumb on it, we dropped some particles of lime, such as was on the ceiling of the vaults, we dripped water, but nothing would replicate the effect. I can't find an explanation for them.'**

Here are descriptions of some of the most peculiar light anomalies the *Most Haunted* team have come across, followed by their descriptions of occasions on which they think they might just possibly have seen a ghost.

Culzean Castle, Ayrshire

Culzean (pronounced 'cullane') Castle was an ancestral towerhouse dating back to 1165. Between 1777 and 1792, David, 10th Earl of Kennedy, commissioned Robert Adam, the greatest architect of his day, to create an elegant castellated mansion on the site. With such a long history, there are many dramatic stories attached to Culzean, like that of the piper who was sent to play the bagpipes in the underground tunnel system to prove there weren't any ghosts – but never returned. Several witnesses have heard ghostly parties and many have seen a beautiful lady in the top rooms. When Derek arrived, he could hear ghostly violins playing uplifting dance music, and in the Earl's Bedroom he identified a young lady, about 17 to 21 years old, wearing a beautiful ballgown.

When the time came to split off into small groups for the night vigil, it was decided that the girls should sit in the Earl's Bedroom, since

a female ghost might be more likely to contact other women. Sure enough, some extraordinary lights began to travel across the painting of Suzanne Kennedy on one wall, and all the girls saw them with the naked eye, not just through a lens. There was a large round orb and a long thread-like one, glowing like the filament inside an electric bulb, both bigger than any orbs the team have seen, either before or since. The lights seemed to respond to Yvette's excitement and as she asked **'Can you do that for us again?'**, they got even more magnificent, flickering and shimmering as if 'Suzanne' wanted to give her visitors a very special show.

A light anomaly travels across the portrait of Suzanne Kennedy in the Earl's Bedroom.

Tutbury Castle, Staffordshire

Even older than Culzean, Tutbury was first built in 1070, and its walls have sheltered many famous people since then, most notably some British monarchs. Charles I stayed here for a time during the Civil War, before Cromwell caught and executed him. Mary Queen of Scots was imprisoned here three times and loathed it, calling it 'a **vile place exposed to all the winds and injuries of heaven**'. There have been witch burnings and a massacre here over the centuries, and it seemed to be extremely active, with more than 250 ghost sightings recorded between 2000 and 2003.

When there are visitors to the castle, the curator, Leslie Smith, puts on a dress that was owned by Mary Queen of Scots and reads one of her speeches, in the hope of tempting Mary herself to appear. When the *Most Haunted* team filmed her doing this, they captured some orbs moving around the dress as she spoke. But it was upstairs in the Great Hall, next to the much-feared King's Bedroom, that Yvette and Phil Whyman were to get the fright of their lives.

First of all, Yvette volunteered to do a solitary vigil in the bedroom, a room supposedly so haunted that they have had to close it to the public, because so many people were passing out and getting badly affected. However, Yvette didn't feel there was much going on in there until the door closed of its own accord – and that was enough. She has a bit of a phobia about doors closing, so she hurried through to join Phil in the Great Hall. There they noticed some peculiar noises – amongst them a regular tapping sound on the window pane, as though someone

Curator Leslie Smith in a dress owned by Mary Queen of Scots.
The team saw spirit lights around her.

was throwing stones at it. Karl and the team who were downstairs ran outside to search the grounds, but there was no one there. Meanwhile, Yvette began to feel freezing cold, she sensed something blowing in her ear and Phil noticed some spirit lights dancing around her. They were blue-tinged, flashing with tiny halos, which is one way the team could tell when they looked back at the footage that they came from a light source rather than a fault on the tape. You don't get halos from flaws on tape.

Have a look at the footage of the spirit lights at Tutbury Castle some time, if you haven't seen them already. It's hard to imagine what they could be – except a lonely female spirit trying to make contact with Yvette … **'I genuinely felt there was a presence there in the room with us,'** she says.

OUTDOOR LIGHTS

There are a number of theories to explain ghostly lights seen outdoors. Could they be caused by natural gases escaping from the earth, or an electromagnetic or 'earth energy' causing phosphoresence? Are they the ignis fatuus or will-o'-the-wisp of folk tales, sent to lure unwary travellers to their deaths? Or could they be spirits visiting a place they are attracted to and trying to draw our attention to it?

The magnificent Chillingham Castle.

Chillingham Castle, Northumberland

The licence to build this crenellated fortress was issued in 1344 and it was remodelled in the seventeenth century. The current occupants, Sir Humphrey Wakefield and his family, have got used to coexisting with all the spirit presences in their home but their dog, Billy, still growls into a particular corner. This was the first place where Karl and Yvette filmed after the pilot, and they immediately felt daunted when they heard a fierce hissing sound, like an aggressive snake, as soon as they walked through the door. There were no pipes, no central heating system; the Wakefields said it happens all the time at that spot and staff refuse to go into that corridor off the main hall.

Derek and Yvette in the passageway at Chillingham Castle, said to be haunted by a Blue Boy.

JUST PASSING THROUGH

At Chillingham Castle, the spirit of a woman called Mary who doesn't like men passed straight through Rick Fielding, telling Derek that he reminded her of her hated ex-husband, who had run off with her sister. Rick's eyes glazed over and became bloodshot, then he started swaying from side to side and, as he fell, he dropped a £20,000 camera on the ground. It's a disturbing experience when a spirit comes inside your aura, according to Derek. Some people simply feel a rise in body temperature but Rick felt a good deal more than that. He was very unwell afterwards, and Derek had to tell Mary to leave him alone.

One of the most common sightings at Chillingham Castle is of a 'Blue Boy' – so-called because visitors see a distinctive blue flash going through the wall just outside a room known as the Pink Bedroom. This flash has been seen countless times over the years by people who knew nothing of previous sightings, so the team were keen to find out if Derek would pick up anything in that corridor.

Rick Fielding collapsed and dropped his camera on the stairs at Chillingham Castle.

When they got upstairs, Derek felt disorientated, he said, as if he was surrounded by a pink, swirling mist. He walked into the passageway and described a boy with a blue aura around him, a strong healing colour that was helping him to come into our atmosphere. Derek channelled the Blue Boy to let him speak, and he cried: **'Leave me alone … Someone help me … Behind the wall … Man locked here with me …**

I didn't want him here.' It turns out that a boy's body had been found behind that wall in the early 1900s, with a man's body alongside him. Derek helped that boy to go into the light, to be with his mother, and the corridor felt much more peaceful afterwards.

Drury Lane Theatre, London

Actors tend to have lots of superstitions, such as telling colleagues to 'break a leg' on first nights and never mentioning Shakespeare's 'Scottish play' by name. One belief is that it's lucky to have a resident ghost in the theatre where you're working. In that case, Drury Lane must be one of the luckiest theatres in the world, because at least five ghosts have been spotted there – one (or maybe two) of them by Yvette.

First, Yvette and Jason Karl saw a figure of a man carrying loads of chains, who crossed the end of the corridor they were standing in. They assumed he was an employee but when the team searched the building they couldn't find anyone resembling him for love nor money. When they played back the sound recording of the incident, you can quite clearly hear rattling chains.

Then, Yvette, Jason and Rick saw a pair of legs on the stairs. It was very clear and their accounts are remarkably similar. '**I know what I saw,**' Yvette remembers, '**and there isn't a logical explanation for it. There was definitely something there, but what? A grounded spirit? A replay of energy in time, like a video channel playing in the building?**'

What they should have done straight away is go to separate rooms and describe what they had seen into diary camcorders, then compare

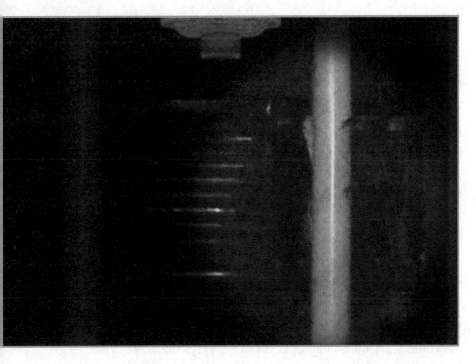

The shadowy figure by the stairs at the Drury Lane Theatre.

their accounts to check whether they had all experienced the same thing. But this was the first series and they were still honing their investigative techniques. Never mind!

An earlier photographer caught an image of a shadowy man, just by the staircase where they saw the legs, although he swears there was no one there at the time. Check it out and see what you think. Is it an actor passing by just as the camera has slipped out of focus? Or is it a male spirit in a Dick Turpin-style hat and long black leather boots, with a ponytail down his back? Could this have been the same spirit that Yvette, Jason and Rick thought they saw?

Belgrave Hall, Leicester

It was at this Georgian country house that Stuart Torevell saw his first ghost. Here's his description: **'Rick and I were sitting on a bench outside, getting a breath of fresh air. Just in front of us there was a brick wall, about 10 feet high, and I saw a bright shape moving along it. There were no legs, just a side profile, and I couldn't even tell you if it was male or female. I'd say it was about 5 feet, 5 inches tall and moving at a slow walking speed. Before I could turn to Rick and say "Will you look at that!", it was gone. Probably it had been there about 20 seconds. Just minutes before, I'd given my camera to Karl so he could carry on filming upstairs. It's always the way!'**

CORNER-OF-THE-EYE PHENOMENON

The normal field of vision for someone looking straight ahead, with their head up, is 130°. When it's dark, peripheral vision widens because the rods and cones (visual receptors) inside the eye adjust, trying to pick up as much light as they can. Fear can also cause the pupils to dilate, as you instinctively search for an escape route. Maybe this is why so many ghost sightings are described as 'out of the corner of the eye'.

Stuart saw a bright shape moving along a wall outside Belgrave Hall.

It was in the same garden that some famous footage purporting to show a ghost (or ghosts) was captured on CCTV. The security camera in the grounds was triggered by a fox, then you see two white figures near the living-room window and a grey ball of light travelling along the wall. Experts who've examined the footage think the shapes could be a falling leaf of some kind and, since the show aired, investigators have concluded that the grey ball of light was a spider. But it's strange that the CCTV cameras captured such unusual effects close to where Stuart saw *his* ghost. (There's more on this lively place, where the team were joined by Vic Reeves and Nancy Sorrell, in Chapter 11.)

RAF East Kirkby, Lincolnshire

This Second World War airfield is now home to a museum of aircraft and memorabilia of the period – and, if locals are to be believed, to several ghosts of airmen who died in the vicinity. (You'll find the full story in Chapter 12.) The owner's son, Jonathan, joined the team for their terrifying vigil among the charred remains of burned-out planes, and he was standing next to Karl when they both saw a shadowy figure.

Karl recalls: '**It was a dark outline, but I could see he was wearing a cap and appeared to be in uniform. He was just 6 feet away from us and pointing to the left, as if at a plane. I said to Jonathan, "Look!", and he said, "I see it!", and we both described the same thing. Yes, I know we should have gone off and told our stories separately, but you don't always do the best thing in the heat of the moment.**'

Psychic Art

According to David, mediums see spirits with a third eye in their minds. He explains: '**Imagine a lemon. Now imagine cutting it open. Think of the smell, the taste. You should find that your mouth is watering. It all forms a connection and comes together into a kind of composite picture. When I'm seeing a picture, the clarity depends on the spirit themselves. Sometimes they are too clear. For example, the spirits of an old man and an old woman live in my house, and I often find myself apologizing for bumping into them on the stairs or disturbing them when I open the door of a room they're in!**'

Derek says: 'I see a figure with varying degrees of clarity, depending on how much effort the spirit person puts in and how well they've learned the technique. It can be an outline of lights, or an outline with some features filled in, maybe just from the chest up, or the ones who've really developed their technique will show details like the colour of their eyes and facial expressions.'

Brian Shepherd is an artist who found that he could see spirit people. Here's his description of how he works: 'I like to walk around the building on my own as soon as I arrive, to open up my mind and free myself, so I can be receptive. When I hit a spot that feels better than any other, I will sit down and begin to doodle. Sometimes nothing will

Brian Shepherd sketching in the attic at Chatham Dockyard.

come at all; at other times it feels like I'm being guided. At first, it's a feeling about the essence of a person, then the shape of a nose, the eyes, whatever. Sometimes it's just a head and the rest of the figure is blurred. An outline comes at first, then more detail.

'I work in charcoal because it's more graphic, has more power. I don't use colour. If I had to stop and think, "Am I getting a facial tone through?", it would be too much. I want to create something very powerful. Some portraits look shallow and you feel as though you're missing something about the person. I strive to capture the essence.'

At Chatham Dockyard in Kent, a 400-year-old naval base where Nelson's ship HMS *Victory* was built, Brian was drawn to the attic. 'I got visions of a young lady at a window but, as I sat, I could see her going from the window through to a cupboard on the landing. She was lifting bedding from the cupboard, tidying it, as though she was busy making up beds, then she walked back to the window and I saw she had a piece of rope in her hands. She was looking out to sea in a wistful, hopeless way, and I got the impression she was waiting for her lover to come back but was losing hope.' Brian drew his image of the girl and showed it to the team. It was only later that they told him a young girl had hanged herself on the rickety old stairs leading up to the attic because her lover hadn't come back from sea.

His drawings astonish residents and eyewitnesses at the locations. At the Black Swan Inn in Devizes, Wiltshire, the landlady seemed sceptical when Brian arrived with his sketchpad. 'I can only do what I do,' Brian says. 'I got an image of a chap sitting by the bar, like some

Brian's drawing of a spirit at the Black Swan.

old local, so that's what I drew. He had a hat and a bulbous kind of nose. As soon as she saw it, the landlady burst into tears. It hit a chord with her that I had seen the same as she had been seeing over the years.' It turns out the spirit is quite a regular in their bar, seen by the landlady and various members of staff. He sometimes appears so real that the landlady will ask her employees, **'Have you served him yet?'**

In an upstairs bedroom at the Black Swan, Brian also drew a picture of a young lady who was pregnant or had just lost a child. Once again this rang true with the landlady, and she related a story she'd heard about a woman who had died in childbirth in that room.

'It was a very fruitful night,' Brian recalls, **'and I got a phone call from the landlady later wanting copies of my drawings.'**

The pictures Brian drew at the *Most Haunted* shoots at Craig y Nos, the Ancient Ram Inn and Maes Artro come later in the book. In the next chapter, we're going to visit a very strange smugglers' inn, right in the heart of Cornwall, where both Yvette and Cath Howe thought they might have seen a spirit.

CHAPTER 8

Jamaica Inn,
Cornwall

Smuggling was one of the mainstays of the Cornish economy during the eighteenth and nineteenth centuries. The long, twisting coastline of the peninsula, with its hidden bays, underground caves and tunnel systems, made it an ideal place to bring ashore kegs of liquor, crates of tobacco, rifles, fine silks for ladies' gowns and any other goods for which customs would otherwise have charged import duty. The smugglers then had to transport their contraband across the bleak expanse of Bodmin Moor and on to where their customers awaited in the towns of southern England.

In 1750, an inn was erected in an isolated spot just near the turnpike between Launceston and Bodmin, to give travellers a place to rest overnight – no questions asked. Its reputation grew until it became a notorious hangout for all kinds of travelling criminals, and with such rough and ruthless types as residents there were bound to be unsavoury and disturbing incidents. Novelist Daphne du Maurier heard some of the local lore and immortalized the inn in her 1936 novel *Jamaica Inn*.

There was a full moon when the *Most Haunted* team arrived to carry out their investigation one wintry evening. Would this mean that there were more spirits in the atmosphere? Would it make everyone more jumpy than usual? They would need to keep their collective nerve as the night wore on and it appeared as though different spirit residents of the inn were coming forward to make themselves known …

Guests who stayed in room 4 had often reported wakening in the night to see a highwayman in a green coat and tricorn hat or to hear horses whinnying in the yard and coaches crunching across gravel – even though the inn now has a cobbled not a gravel courtyard. When Derek arrived in room 4, he picked up on 'a big fella, with a strange hat, a long cloak and boots. He's a hoarder … a smuggler … I see kegs and wooden boxes pushed together.' Derek identified this man as Jack Trevellis, and said he was 'well known in Polperro before the authorities took his life'. He also mentioned the date 1791, but Richard's research has been unable to verify the existence of this man.

In room 5, previous guests had seen a ghostly woman and child walking through the wall, almost as if they were coming out of a mirror that hung there. The story is that a woman stayed there with her son the night before catching a boat at Falmouth, which sank and drowned them both. The *Most Haunted* team witnessed a lot of activity in this room – not all of which was shown in the episode that aired.

First of all, Cath saw something. 'I was sitting on the bed next to Derek, and Phil [Whyman] and Simon [Williams] had cameras. I saw a shadow that ran along the wall, about 3 feet tall, like the shape of a child. It was a black outline, kind of like those black silhouettes that you see at the end of the film *Ghost*. I said to the others, "Did you see that?", and Derek said, "Yes", and traced with his finger along exactly the route I'd seen the figure running.'

Richard Felix, Jon Dibley, soundman Tom O'Carroll and locations manager Wendy James also saw strange shadows in room 5, and a door kept opening on its own despite the fact that there was no draught, so they called in Yvette and guest medium Ian Lawman. As soon as Ian arrived, he saw a figure running through the door that kept opening. Then Yvette caught something strange as she directed her camera at the mirror the woman was supposed to walk through. **'I saw the face of a woman looking out at me through the mirror. She was wearing a bonnet, tied under her chin, and to me it was very exciting. That's the closest I've come to seeing a ghost, apart from the legs at Drury Lane. There were little lights coming out of the mirror just at the place where her face was.'**

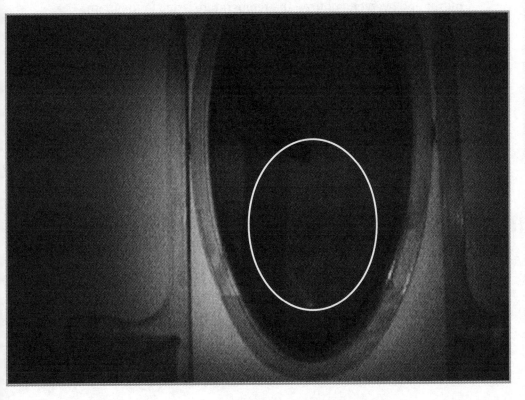

Is there a woman's face in the mirror?

At that point, Ian began to channel the woman and let her tell her story. '**I wouldn't let him in but he made me … He didn't pay me,**' she said. It seems she was a lady of the night, and one particular customer had raped and then strangled her. This tied in with what Derek had sensed earlier, that a woman had been murdered, and he further suggested that the murderer had been the innkeeper. Ian became very emotional as he told her story, and seemed to feel her pain as the man put his fingers round her throat. '**She was a lady in trauma,**' he says. '**She needed to be put to rest. I specialize in spirits who need to be rescued – it's the area I feel most comfortable with – so I led her towards the light, reassuring her that she was safe now and no one could hurt her any more.**' Afterwards, the face had gone from the mirror and everyone noticed the temperature rising in the room.

The Generator Room

This is the part of the inn where staff refuse point-blank to go at night, and they will only venture down in twos or threes during daylight hours. Stuart describes it: '**It's old and rusty, full of broken stuff, empty baked-bean cans with nails in them, cobwebs, rotting beams and stuff that was put there years ago.**' Derek pointed up to the rafters and told the team that brothers John and James Broad, eighteenth-century innkeepers, had been duped by a man, so John had hanged him from that very rafter. When Yvette looked up, she saw white shapes in the old rafters: '**Like a long shadowy body shape with a head, but not clear like the woman's face in the mirror had been.**'

The moment when something touched Stuart's back in the generator room.

At that moment, someone or something began to throw things at the crew, and they seemed to be coming from the rafters. First it was a metallic object, possibly an old nail, and then some muck fell on Yvette's face. They challenged the spirit, saying '**If you don't want us here, give us a sign and we'll leave**'. And each time they said it, something was thrown or there was a noise.

Stuart says: '**When things started being thrown, the film crew didn't know where to point a camera. They were coming from all** directions, so it couldn't possibly have been one person faking it.' They got more and more jumpy until suddenly there was a crash that startled them all and something touched Stuart. '**It was a firm pressure across my shoulderblades, like claws,**' he remembers. But there was no one standing behind him – at least no one visible.

That was enough. Everyone turned and ran screaming outside. Yvette hurt herself in her panic. '**I jammed my shin against a piece of machinery. You just think, "Something's going to get me", and you run.**' Outside in the courtyard, Richard heard the crash and the mass panic and got almost as much of a fright as those inside. '**I heard people yelling and then they all came charging out and I didn't have a clue what was going on. It was utterly terrifying.**'

You'd think that would be enough for one night and they'd agree to steer well clear of the generator room from then on. As far as viewers saw when the episode went out on air, that was it. But it wasn't …

Ouija Boards

Unbelievably, Karl, Yvette, Stuart and Ian returned to the generator room to try to contact the spirit there using a ouija board. This wasn't shown at the time, because the team have mixed feelings about ouija boards – and also because what the spirit said was so violent and horrible.

'**Basically, it wanted to kill Karl,**' Stuart recalls. '**We could hear rusty old chains rattling in the distance and the lock-off camera we'd positioned down the table caught the sound.**' Yvette remembers it telling them all to '****** off and die**'.

Here's a cross section of the team's feelings about ouija boards:

- Derek has very strong views: 'I think they're barbaric. Why do people use them instead of communicating through mediums? How can you trust that a communicator is who they purport to be? Do they come from the lower regions? What's dangerous is when a negative energy realizes that there's an undeveloped mind, doing it for fun, and they can prey on their energy. Just one energy is bad enough, because they might decide to stay and feed like a vampire for days to come and bad things could happen to that person. But what if several negative energies arrive at once? Then you'd have problems. Those people's lives could be harmed for months, unless they sought the help of a medium to deal with it.'

- This happened to Stuart: 'Years ago, I had a bad experience with a ouija board. I couldn't sleep afterwards because I was crying, shaking and in so much pain. My stomach hurt, legs hurt; I had a migraine, toothache and earache all at once. I always put it down to using the ouija board and I've been careful with them ever since.'

- David says: 'Ouija boards are certainly dangerous, and we wouldn't use them on the show without a medium in the building.'

- Yvette says: 'We have to try these things, because our aim is to investigate the paranormal from every angle. Whenever I've done it, I'm sure the pointer moved by itself without anyone pushing it. There was some kind of energy there, but I don't know how it works. They've got this huge stigma now from books and films, but my feeling is that if it works and is true, it could be useful.'

- Karl says it's just a game. He's got a ouija board in the office that is sold as a board game for kids aged eight and over. '**People are so desperate for the pointer to move that they create subconscious micro-muscular movements, but it's misleading. If they do it in daylight, it spells out names and answers questions and so forth, but try doing it in the dark and the glass just falls off the table. If it worked in the dark, I'd say, "Fair enough!"**' Then he adds: '**Anyway, a lot of spirits you contact from past centuries wouldn't have been able to read or write or know the alphabet, so they wouldn't be able to spell things out.**'

The *Most Haunted* team prefer divination with a glass to the use of ouija boards. (There's more about this in Chapter 13.)

YES OR NO

Ouija boards were invented in 1892 by American Elija J. Bond, and their name came from the words for 'yes' in French and German ('*oui*' + '*ja*'). The letters of the alphabet, numbers 0 to 9 and the words 'yes' and 'no' are arranged around the pointer. They became very popular during and after the First World War, when thousands wanted to contact the husbands and sons they had lost.

The Jamaica Inn: peaceful again in daylight.

Back to Room 5

At 6 a.m., Stuart and Rick packed the kit away and stopped to have a couple of beers with the owners of the Jamaica Inn, who were in the bar. Stuart recalls: '**We heard this almighty scraping above us, like furniture being moved around, and the owners told us, "That's room 5." Seemingly, at that time every morning they hear the sound of furniture being moved, but when you go up there and open the door, nothing is out of place. Unfortunately, we didn't have a** camera and tape recorder because everything had been packed away.

'The noise lasted over an hour. Problem was, that was the only room left for Rick and me to sleep in, so we had to go up. From the noise outside the door, it sounded like a party in there, and we expected the curtains to be blowing about, chairs all stacked up, everything topsy turvy. But we opened the door and it was a completely normal hotel bedroom. Rick and I were so shattered that we just went to bed and crashed out.'

CHAPTER 9

What Do Ghosts Sound Like?

'It always seems to be me who's going "What was that? Did you hear that?"' Yvette says. 'I'd worry they would all think I'm going mad, except that I wear a radio mic so nine times out of ten when I hear something, it's been picked up on tape as well. Thank goodness!'

By later series, you'll notice that the team are much less jumpy than they used to be about creaks, bangs and other things that go bump in the night. Their baseline-test research is much more thorough than it used to be, especially since Ciaran got involved in series 4, so they can often pinpoint the source of a noise reasonably quickly. If they're not sure, they'll try to reproduce what they heard in order to figure out what caused it – like the door creaking open in Jamaica Inn. Of course, there are lots they can't explain: the sharp tapping on the window at Tutbury Castle, the fierce hissing at Chillingham Castle, the beer barrels clanging together at Greengate Brewery and many more besides.

On set, radio mics are usually attached to Yvette, Ciaran, Derek and David, then the sound recordist uses a boom mic on a stick to pick up other noises and general background. When people go off on night vigils, they have hand-held camcorders with digital tape recorders to capture the experience. Here are a few of the spookiest noises they've heard:

- 'Of all the noises we hear, I think footsteps are the most freaky,' says Karl. When Karl, Yvette, Richard and David heard footsteps in the next room at the Guildhall, Leicester, they knew they had a problem, because the rest of the team were in completely different parts of the building. Karl says: 'I knew no one else was near us but the footsteps were so loud … I went to look, and noted that the floor was concrete, but there was no one there. What scares you is that you can hear something walking towards you but your eyes tell you there's nothing there.' Rachel Philips also heard footsteps later, when she was with Karl and Derek. 'They were so clear, and I could feel the floor vibrating as though someone was walking across it.'

- At Maes Artro, in north-west Wales, Ciaran was particularly impressed by the footsteps they all heard walking back and forwards outside the Officers' Mess. 'They weren't just picked up by the human ear,' he says, 'but were recorded by the equipment. I ran outside straight away to check, but there was no one in the vicinity.'

- At Lower Wellhead Farm, in Clitheroe, the team heard doors banging loudly upstairs. Finally, they went to ask the owner what was going on and he pointed out that all the doors had been taken off their hinges in preparation for stripping. They have no idea what could have caused the banging there.

- Karl's other scariest sound was when he heard that voice telling him to 'Get out!' at the Edinburgh Vaults. 'I didn't react straight away. At first I thought it was a member of the crew, although the voice was very deep. Then I realized there was no one near me. In the cold light of day, I thought, "Could it have been clothes rustling, or something else?" That's why we use diary cams on the spot, to capture immediate impressions before cold-light-of-day syndrome sets in.'

- At Arreton Manor, on the Isle of Wight, David and Yvette simultaneously heard monks singing Gregorian chants.

- At Bodelwyddan Castle, in Wales, Rachel and Yvette jumped out of their skins when they heard a deep intake of breath that seemed to come from right beside them. Rachel says: 'It wasn't a nice noise. Yvette screamed and ran, leaving me on my own, and I could feel breath on my face.'

- Yvette hates to hear breathing in her ear. 'Breathing frightens me, because if it's real, then it's very close by, and we've found out through our filming that ghosts can actually harm you. Who would lean over and breathe in your ear just to get your attention? What sort of person does that? I've often asked David Wells, "Why don't they lean over and say 'Hi' or 'Hello' in a sweet soft voice?" But the problem is that more often than not it's negative people coming through, not the nice ones. Laughter is spooky too. You get back to your hotel and think, "Please God, don't let anything have followed me." And if I heard a spirit speaking to me, I think I'd end up in a rocking chair in a nursing home.'

● The team have often heard what they thought was laughter and have caught it on tape as well. At the Golden Fleece pub, in York, Radio 1 DJ Scott Mills and his team were sitting in on a séance with Yvette and the others. Yvette said, **'Let us know if you don't want us to be here,'** and all of a sudden she heard three distinct sniggering sounds in her ear: **'Huh, huh, huh.'** 'I burst into tears,' she says. **'The others were looking at me like I was a total mad person, but then Jon [Gilbert] played it back to me and you can hear it, clear as anything.'** Ciaran says: **'That laughter is unexplainable. I'm definitely keeping an open mind about it.'**

Why don't ghosts speak to us directly? Derek says that, as with seeing ghosts, the reason we can't hear them clearly is because they exist at a different vibrational level and they have to learn to slow down even to communicate with a medium. Ian Lawman explains what he hears when he speaks to spirits: **'It's like talking to the living but we only catch snippets of the conversation. It's not very clear, like talking on a telephone line with a poor connection, so we can only grab certain bits.'** This is why the mediums can't always provide full names, dates, facts and figures on demand, although they may pick up snatches of information and random phrases.

> ## KEEPING A LOG
>
> During the night vigils, Rachel Philips keeps a log of where everyone is, and she sets off last. Their cameras are all synchronized to the same time and cross-checked. That way, if someone hears footsteps in a room above, Rachel can tell them immediately 'That's Karl and Stuart' or 'Erm, there's no one up there . . .' When they check the footage later, the time logs and the cameras' time codes confirm where everyone was at any given time.

Infrasound

Some physicists at Coventry University are researching a theory that low-frequency sound, below the range of human hearing (i.e. below 20 hertz), is often found at locations that are said to be haunted. There are several natural phenomena that can cause infrasound: thunderstorms, earthquakes and tidal waves are examples. Well before the Asian tsunami hit the coast on 26 December 2004, most birds and animals had headed for higher ground. Many experts think they heard the infrasound created by the underwater earthquake or picked up the distant tremors in time to save themselves.

Elephants, hippos, capercaillies and some species of whale are particularly responsive to infrasound. Elephants and hippos find a safe spot to lie down when a thunderstorm is approaching, long before humans have detected a change in the weather. Even cows sense the approach of rain before we do, and will choose a sheltered patch in their field to rest and wait it out.

In cars travelling at high speeds, infrasound can have adverse effects on drivers, causing headaches, loss of concentration and drowsiness. However, some cats purr at infrasound levels and this can have a soothing effect on human beings, vibrating throughout the body.

In houses, sources of infrasound can include the hum of an air-conditioning unit, or wind whistling through an enclosed area or any number of low-level vibrational phenomena. Researchers have documented a range of symptoms when subjects are put in a room that contains infrasound: they feel sick, experience pressure in their heads, get tingling spines and a sense that there's 'someone there'. There are some locations where the Most Haunted team have all reported feeling sick, and Karl in particular seems to be very prone to severe headaches. Could these symptoms be explained by infrasound? Derek explains their malaise as caused by them picking up residual energies.

It has often been noted that dogs seem to sense something in haunted properties. At Moresby Hall, in Cumbria, the owner's dog often growls at one corner of the sitting room, and the same is true at Chillingham Castle, in Northumberland. Ian Lawman takes his dog, Billy, for walks along a riverbank and says Billy always goes crazy at one particular point that has been the scene of many local suicides. What can he sense there?

When they took a dog into the attic at Owlpen Manor, it appeared very interested in something in the corner, but in this instance it couldn't have been infrasound the dog was reacting to. That particular dog is stone deaf. (See Chapter 14 for more on Owlpen.)

Electronic Voice Phenomenon (EVP)

Some paranormal researchers claim that they have captured spirit voices on audio tape, and a 2005 film *White Noise*, starring Michael Keaton, explores this phenomenon. Voice experts claim to be able to match the vocal patterns recorded with those of people who died several years earlier – but sceptics always seem to be able to find an alternative explanation. The *Most Haunted* team usually leave a tape recorder running in the room where they've left the trigger object, but they haven't had any conclusive results – yet.

At Brannigan's Nightclub, they left a tape recorder running in the spooky Old Tower, just by the place where Yvette detected a strong smell of baby sick. They were all astonished when they played back the tape to hear an undulating **'weh-weh-weh'** sound, just like a ghostly baby. But did the team think 'baby' just because of the smell earlier? If you had heard that noise without anyone mentioning the word 'baby' to you, is that what you would have decided it was? Or could there have been a natural explanation to do with external noises and the acoustics of the tower?

At the Ancient Ram Inn, Rachel and Alex Lysaght heard a cat miaowing in one room that was said to be haunted, and the owner confirmed that cat noises had been heard there before, although there were no cats on the premises. Ciaran locked-off the room with a camera and an MP3 recorder. Here's what he found: **'When I listened to the tape, about 20 minutes in there was a cat sound. I was so excited I ran to tell Yvette, and everyone listened and agreed that's what it was.**

TVS AND RADIOS

Some people think that spirits can communicate through the white noise of an untuned radio or television. At a live event at London's Midland Grand Hotel, the team tuned a radio to 1475 kHz medium wave, a frequency at which there are no other stations nearby, and left it beside a tape recorder – but all they recorded was white noise. At Craigievar Castle, they thought they could hear voices through the white noise of a radio, but, Ciaran says, 'Your hearing starts to get used to the noise and pick out other distant frequencies.' At the Clockhouse in Surrey, they tried watching an untuned television set and asking the spirits to show them pictures. Karl says: 'You do get images when you ask for them, but is it like seeing faces in the clouds? Until something definite happens, all we've got is an untuned radio and an untuned TV.'

I checked the area thoroughly and there were no ledges, so no way an actual cat could have been there ... Anyway, back at the university I put the cat tape through a spectrograph and was disappointed to see that the wave forms didn't seem to indicate cat noise. I played the tape to several colleagues without telling them what they were listening for, and several of them said that it sounded like a little boy crying out. Sure enough, behind the Ancient Ram Inn there is an area where little boys sometimes play on a trampoline. I was very disappointed.'

Laboratory tests have indicated the power of suggestion when it comes to identifying the source of a noise. A person listening to a range of different sounds will hear more or less what they want to, or whatever has been suggested to them by other visual or olfactory clues or just by their knowledge of the place they are in. But that doesn't prove that they are not hearing a sound created by a spirit; it would just affect the way they interpreted it.

Responding to Requests

There's no doubt that one of the things that scares the team the most is when someone – or something – appears to be replying to their questions or requests. In the generator room at Jamaica Inn and in the basement at Greengate Brewery, objects seemed to be thrown every time the team asked **'Give us a sign if you want us to leave'**. In séances, if they ask a spirit to knock once if they are there, a single knock is often heard.

Ciaran counsels caution, though. He believes that knocking sounds in séances can be caused inadvertently by participants; a ring or piece of jewellery bumping ever so slightly against the table when there's a boom mic nearby can end up sounding just like a deliberate knock. As far as Greengate and Jamaica Inn are concerned, he says, he would need a lock-off camera with a wide angle capturing the object being thrown before he would be convinced. He tells the following, disappointing story.

'At Kinnity Castle, in Ireland, Derek and Richard Felix appeared to be communicating with a spirit and getting bangs in answer to their questions. When they paused, there was no bang. They invited me to witness it and I heard exactly the same thing. When they asked a question, there was a bang, then they paused and there was silence, then they asked another question and there was a bang. I went off to investigate and unfortunately I found the cause next door – a boiler system for a sauna, which was set on a perpetual timer. When it came on, there was a bang, then a pause, then another bang, and the time between the bangs was irregular because of the way the thermostat worked, then there was a slight click and a period of extra silence. As far as Derek and Richard were aware, they were getting a definite response – but it came down to coincidence.'

Certainly there have been plenty of *Most Haunted* experiences that scared the team silly at the time but for which a natural explanation was later found. But there have also been plenty of other weird sounds heard for which they've found no explanations. And there have been all those other sounds heard when the camera and sound recorder weren't set up, so the incident didn't make it into the TV show that aired. We'll explore a couple of bizarre sound-related instances in this chapter before going on, in the next, to a place where *everyone* heard some very unusual noises.

Charleville Forest Castle, County Offaly, Ireland

There's a story attached to this derelict castle that in the 1700s, a young girl who was sliding down the banister fell to her death. Children who visit the castle now often report hearing and seeing her. When *Most Haunted* filmed there, it was Stuart she seemed to want to talk to. '**I was upstairs setting up on my own while everyone else was having lunch. I'm standing on the top of a ladder, running cables and setting up the lights, when I heard a kid laughing. I couldn't see anything but for the next five minutes or so, I kept hearing a little girl talking, laughing and then crying. I wasn't frightened at all – she seemed nice. It was only when I got downstairs that Karl told me a little girl was often seen and heard up there … Later on when I was derigging, she whispered something right into my ear and the hairs on the back of my neck stood up.**'

Croxteth Hall, Liverpool

Brian Shepherd likes to be quite independent on set, walking around, picking up the energies and deciding where to start drawing. He was completely alone when he had the following experience in Croxteth Hall: '**The whole place is quite sinister. It's huge, with lots of bedrooms, and the temperature seems to change dramatically from one part to the** next. There's a room that was damaged by fire in the 1950s and hasn't been redecorated, and I found it quite creepy. When I sat down, a male presence began to come through, a demanding kind of character. I was drawing away when suddenly I heard footsteps and giggling in the corridor; it sounded like two teenage girls. I could imagine them just near the door, wearing Victorian costume, and I turned the page of my sketchpad to try and draw them. However, I was distracted by the male presence saying loudly in my ear: "In my house, you focus on me!" He didn't want anyone else getting my attention.'

Chatham Dockyard, Kent

In the old naval dockyards, the team agreed that the Joiner's Workshop was the eeriest place of all. Everyone got very, very scared there. They had heard about the reports of dark, evil shadows walking towards visitors, of extreme cold spots and people being pushed by unseen hands. Yvette remembers: 'I was absolutely petrified because it was so black, so dark, and the wind was howling outside.'

The strong wind rattling the windows and doorframes meant the team had to do a lot of discounting when they heard spooky noises. Even when all the doors were closed, they still heard banging and clicking sounds, but most were tracked down to a draught getting in somewhere.

When Derek came into the Joiner's Workshop, he identified a nuisance spirit person who was causing poltergeistal activity. 'He's a soldier in uniform ... a bad one ... he's killed an innocent person. He re-energizes at this level although he doesn't belong here.' In the

To this day, Yvette counts the Joiner's Workshop at Chatham Dockyard as one of the scariest places she's investigated.

séance later, Derek identified him as Richard Neville, but no records of this name can be found.

Tension mounted when something hit the back of Brian Shepherd's head, then Tom O'Carroll felt a strong, isolated gust of wind – or a push – on the back of his coat. But the scariest thing for Yvette was a distinctive dragging sound. '**I don't know what it was. We tried to re-enact it but nothing would work**.' Richard Felix suggested that a draught might have rustled some dead leaves in the corner of the room, but no amount of effort could make those leaves sound like the heavy dragging sound they captured on tape. It sounded like a heavy load being pulled across the wooden floorboards – perhaps something as heavy as a dead body.

Later, Karl went back for a lone vigil in the Workshop and he heard exactly the same dragging sound. Was it the spirit of the soldier, Richard Neville, getting rid of the body of someone he'd murdered? Or was it an auditory illusion? Listen to the episode yourself and decide …

CHAPTER 10

Craig y Nos, Powys

Craig y Nos (the name means 'Rock of the Night') was originally built by local landowner Captain Rice Powell in 1842, but after opera-singer Adelina Patti bought it in 1878, she undertook such an extensive remodelling that it quadrupled in size. Among other features, she added castellated turrets and a 200-seat theatre where she could entertain her rich and famous friends. By this time, Adelina was married to her second

Adelina Patti's house.

The inscription over the stage in the theatre Adelina built.

husband, a French tenor called Ernesto Nicolini, but the great love of her life had died a decade earlier in 1868.

Gioacchino Antonio Rossini, the renowned composer of *The Barber of Seville*, *William Tell* and many other great operas, had been a very close friend of Adelina's. Yvette explains: '**No one has said explicitly that they had an affair but it's definitely implied that they did. She admired him more than anyone else. She was in awe of him.**' When Rossini died, Adelina collapsed in shock, and her final request was to be buried next to him. When she died in 1919, at the age of 79, after falling down some stairs in the house, she was initially embalmed in the cellar, then taken to Paris and buried with her beloved Rossini. However, this reunion was only to last a few years before his body was interred and moved, so now she rests alone. Could this be why she won't leave

Craig y Nos, the place she loved so much? Derek says: **'She will move on when she wants to, but she's chosen to be there for now.'**

When Brian Shepherd sat drawing in Adelina's theatre, he sensed a male presence with her. **'They were as one, coming together, and I got a very strong feeling that they were romantically attached.'** Brian sat alone in the theatre for quite some time before he felt the figures coming through. **'I was embarrassed because it was the first time I'd been on *Most Haunted* and I didn't think I was going to get anything. I tried three times before I managed to draw something I felt reasonably good about. She was talking and I got a feeling of gaiety, that she liked to have people around her, and then this strong male presence muscled in too.'**

Brian Shepherd's sketches of the spirits he sensed in the theatre bear an uncanny resemblance to Rossini and Adelina.

Yvette on Adelina's stage.

Brian couldn't put names to the man and the woman he drew – he had no idea whose house he was in – but the facial lines are very clear and distinctive and there's a quite extraordinary resemblance to Adelina Patti and Rossini. Derek explains: '**Adelina had decided to pose for him, she was happy to do it, and in return he let her close enough to draw on his energy, which she needed to maintain herself in our atmosphere. It's a 50/50 thing.**'

The team were all very keen to contact Adelina, who seemed like a good-hearted woman, so at the end of the evening they held a séance on the stage. They played a recording of 'Home, Sweet Home' that Adelina had made in Craig y Nos 98 years earlier. '**It was surreal sitting there on the stage,**' Jon Dibley recalls, '**and I thought I could smell** lavender, but otherwise nothing much happened for me.' Richard Felix adds: 'The temperature dropped significantly when we played that song, and it felt very emotional, but she didn't want to make her presence known.'

If this had been all that happened in Craig y Nos that night, the team would probably remember it as a pleasant, slightly melancholy place. Instead, you can ask any of them and they'll tell you that it was one of the most frightening shoots they have ever been on, given what happened later, and you'd be hard pushed to find anyone who would ever go back there again.

Being Watched

Adelina isn't the only former resident who is reported to haunt Craig y Nos. After her death, the property was converted into a sanitorium for patients with tuberculosis, an infectious bacterial lung disease that had a very high fatality rate in the days before antibiotics were widely available. The treatment of TB patients was often quite drastic. Fresh, clean, cold air was thought to help them breathe, so sanatorium patients at Craig y Nos were frequently made to sleep outside on a balcony or in a kind of summerhouse with a roof but no walls. Those that survived the night were allowed to shuffle back inside; the rest were buried.

Throughout their night vigil, members of the *Most Haunted* team kept hearing heavy breathing, sighing and murmuring in different parts of the property, and they captured some very strange sighing and breathing noises on tape:

- Down in the embalming room in the cellar, Cath Howe, Suzanne Vinton and Wendy James heard breathing noises, as though something was behind them, and they captured an orb on camera.

- Yvette, Richard and Phil Whyman heard breathing and a sound like a man murmuring in the first-floor corridor.

- Karl, Stuart and Phil kept hearing an unexplained banging, along with breathing sounds, and they saw what Stuart called **'flashy things'** in the theatre.

- Tom O'Carroll caught a sound on tape that is exactly like a sigh or an exhalation of breath.

- Karl, Yvette, Phil and Tom heard what they took to be a laugh, once again in the first-floor corridor.

- As they did a lone vigil in Adelina's Boudoir, Karl and Stuart captured a very strange noise on tape, a kind of **'Vrrrooop!'** sound. It has the acoustic properties of the room, so they know it's not an electrical fault, but they have no idea what it could be.

It's as if the very fabric of the old building was breathing on them, with whisperings and sighings coming from all directions. Most of the team say they felt uneasy soon after arriving at Craig y Nos. **'It felt sinister, and very chilled, in a state of disrepair,'** says Brian. Yvette still calls it **'one of the eeriest places I've been to'**.

Soon after his arrival, Derek picked up a story which is not recorded anywhere but, if true, is one of the most terrible things imaginable: he could sense a mother throwing her child from a second-floor window in

Did a mother throw her little boy from this window?

a fit of temper. '**A little boy,**' he said, '**aged between three and seven years old.**' Shortly afterwards, cameraman Simon Williams began to feel unwell, and was clearly running a temperature and sweating, with red blotches on his forehead. Derek told him that a spirit had chosen him as an energy source. '**Usually it's me, but he's chosen you. I can see it.**' And then Derek was hit on the neck by something, while the others heard the sound of laughter. It was clear this spirit wasn't the friendly type.

When they returned to the same spot once the lights were out, Yvette was spooked from the start. She clung for dear life to Richard and even used the 'f' word after a stair creaked. Her fear level just seemed to increase with every step. '**This is the most creepy experience. Jesus! This is bloody horrible, this is nasty,**' she said. They had no idea who or what was making them feel so petrified, although Derek had identified a negative spirit called Vincenti on the lower levels. **'Some places just get to you more than others,'** Yvette sighs. **'I don't know why Craig y Nos was one of them.'**

Downstairs, Karl and Phil spent a lot of time experimenting with doors to see if they could find out what was causing the sporadic, very loud bangs that were making people jump out of their skin – but to no avail. Even the normally unflappable Karl admitted to being **'concerned'** when he and Stuart did the vigil in Adelina's Boudoir.

The temperature dropped so much that the hairs on the backs of their necks were standing up, and it was pitch black. Stuart said, **'You can put your hand in front of your face and you can't see it. It's not a**

Karl and Stuart felt a distinct presence in the room during their vigil in Adelina's Boudoir.

GHOSTLY SCENTS

When the team smell a strong, inexplicable scent in a
location, they should really separate and record their
impressions on diary cams, because once one person has
said out loud what they think it is, they are bound to
influence the others. Everyone could smell a sweetish
scent in Brannigan's Tower but it was Yvette, as the only
mother in the group, who identified it as baby sick. In
Derby Gaol's most active cell, there was a strong smell
of roses, and Jason Karl tried to check whether anyone
was wearing perfume - but, of course, body lotions,
deodorants and even fabric conditioners lingering in
clothing could have produced something similar. However,
like most ghostly scents, it was strong for a few seconds
and then disappeared completely, which wouldn't be
consistent with odour trapped in fibre. Several people
smelled lavender in the theatre at Craig y Nos, and
tobacco smoke has often been detected in an area where
no one has been smoking - Oldham Coliseum and Souter
Lighthouse are two examples. And it has to be said that
they don't always agree on smells. During a séance at
Aberglasney House, Yvette detected a sweet, pretty
perfume, but when Karl leaned over to sniff, he thought it
smelled utterly foul!

Yvette can't explain what made Craig y Nos so terrifying.

nice place to be at all.' Karl heard a footstep. Something fell from the ceiling. There were light anomalies and fairly distinct noises, but what got to them most of all was an overwhelming feeling that they weren't alone in that room. Karl tried to stay practical, using the dim glow from the mini-cam to look for a source of the noise, but Stuart had had his fill. **'I want out!'** he said. **'That's it. Enough's enough.'**

Was the team's foreboding infectious, like the TB bacteria that used to hang heavy in the atmosphere there? Did each set the others off in an escalating scale of panic? Or were they picking up the residual energies of the TB victims, the mother who killed her son in a fit of temper and the mysterious Vincenti in the cellar?

'There's no doubt that something was with us most of the time we were there,' says Richard, 'following us, watching us and frightening us off.' (For more on the 'fear factor', see Chapter 16.)

Room 36

The night before filming started, Richard had a very disturbing experience in room 36 of an annexe of Craig y Nos that has been turned into a hotel. 'When I got there, it was late on a typical winter's day and the place was pitch black, derelict and very cold. I went to bed and woke up at 4 a.m., when I found myself by a wall looking through a door. All I knew was that I didn't like what was through that door. Now, I've never sleepwalked in my life, and I definitely wasn't dreaming. I turned around to see something that looked like a woman lying diagonally across the bed. I was shocked to the core and felt a tingling up my spine and into my neck. I forced myself to go over to the bed and put my hands on it to prove there was nothing there. Then I tried to reshape the bedcovers to see if they could have formed the shape I had seen, but I couldn't re-create it.

'The next day, I was told that two trainee nurses who had slept in that room saw something that looked like snowflakes coming out of the ceiling and they fled, petrified. Later still, I found out that Adelina Patti's private chapel, where her body lay in state, was next door to room 36. In fact, in those days, the chapel may have extended into that space.

'The next night, after we finished the vigil, I had to go back to stay in that room again, but I waited over an hour on set for Phil Whyman to finish his interviews to camera so I wouldn't have to go on my own. To let you know how scared I was, it was after that night that I started wearing a crucifix and I've worn one ever since. It just seems that the longer I work on *Most Haunted*, the more is happening to me.'

CHAPTER 11

Transference

We have all experienced the sensation at one time or another of walking into a building or a particular room and feeling uneasy or anxious for no obvious reason. Maybe there's an oppressive atmosphere or an almost undetectable smell – or perhaps there is a high level of electro-magnetism or infrasound present. Or is there another explanation to do with events that have occurred in that place in the past? Could 'sick building syndrome', where an unusually high number of people working there get ill, have something to do with the building's residual energies? Or is it just caused by faulty air-conditioning systems, toxic materials used in the construction or a lack of natural light?

Certain members of the *Most Haunted* team seem particularly prone to emotional swings, feeling sick, faint and getting headaches. Ciaran has recently been testing their 'magic ideation', or ways of looking at the world creatively, by examining their background belief systems and judging how they tend to react to their environment. They have all filled out questionnaires similar to the one shown on the next page to help him assess which of the team might be more prone to interpret occurrences as paranormal.

MAGIC IDEATION QUESTIONNAIRE

Answer true or false to each of the following:

1. I often worry that I have said or done something I shouldn't have.
2. I believe that coincidences usually mean something.
3. I sometimes feel a sense of impending danger for no obvious reason.
4. I frequently make decisions based on instinct.
5. Sometimes I become aware of strong smells that have no obvious source.
6. I'm very sensitive to criticism and prone to feeling a failure.
7. My moods can change from one minute to the next.
8. On occasion I have felt an overwhelming sense of emptiness.
9. I have sometimes felt as though my voice is very far away when I'm speaking.
10. I have vivid dreams that often wake me in the night.
11. I am prone to daydreaming at work.
12. I think that accidents or bad things can happen for a reason.
13. Occasionally I have looked in the mirror and thought my face looked different.
14. I don't like feeling as though people are watching me.
15. Sometimes, lying in bed, I feel as though my body is a different shape, i.e. longer, fatter or thinner.

The more 'trues', the more likely it is that you have the kind of temporal lobe lability that will be sensitive to high EMF and infrasound.

The theory is that those who have a certain kind of 'temporal lobe lability' (the amount of spontaneous electrical activity in the temporal lobes of their brains) are much more likely to hallucinate or feel unwell when EMF readings are high or when there is infrasound present. If it is proved that people with those kinds of brain are more affected, can we somehow reproduce the results in different conditions? And how would this reflect on the team's experiences in some of the supposedly haunted properties they have investigated?

Ciaran has concluded: '**For particular people, nausea and head-aches, a tingling in the spine and a feeling that someone else is present can be attributed to infrasound. High EMF readings definitely cause symptoms in those who are susceptible as well. Some of the strong emotions the team have experienced have involved the power of suggestion.** [They had been told stories about the property and were already upset or disturbed by them.] **But after Yvette's experiences in hundreds of locations now, I am amazed that some affect her so strongly and she has such an intense reaction, while other equally disturbing ones don't have that effect. It definitely makes me think there's something more to it.**'

How do the mediums explain it? Derek says: '**I can feel negativity from 50 feet away and I can always sense if there's something not very good on the other side of a doorway. I feel a kind of anxiety or depression and know to prepare myself … I've noticed that the** *Most Haunted* **team are becoming much more sensitized from one series to the next. It's a natural progression. If you're open to energies and keep taking yourself to places that have them, things will happen.**'

Derek picking up energies from the spirit world.

Derek continues: '**Sometimes spirits want to communicate with the living in order to relay what happened to them, in a search for justice. They can't always express it in words, so they might try to pass on the emotions and sensations associated with their experience.**' You might see a medium clutch their throat before explaining that a particular person died by hanging. Derek felt palpitations in the Midland Grand Hotel on the spot where George Gilbert Scott's grandson died of a heart attack. David found it difficult to speak after he was approached by a female spirit who was demonstrating to him that her throat had been cut.

According to them, when the *Most Haunted* team members feel suddenly depressed or dizzy, it is because spirits are attempting to show them what they went through. Here are some of their experiences of transference.

Yvette Breaks Down in Derby Gaol

Derby Gaol was opened in 1756 to house all kinds of prisoners, and back in those days, the inmates couldn't be very optimistic about their likely fate. There were over 200 hanging offences in England at the time, including such 'crimes' as impersonating a Chelsea pensioner or setting fire to a haystack. Those who were hanged could dangle for half an hour or more before breathing their last. Even worse, they might still be alive when they were taken down to be drawn and quartered. And this was a better option than being 'gibbeted' – suspended in a metal cage for the crows to pluck their eyes out.

One cell in the gaol seems particularly active. According to Richard Felix, who owns the building, '**Lots of people stop in the doorway and refuse to enter, and those who do go in tend to feel sick and leave fairly quickly. A builder who was working in there was severely traumatized after the door shut on him.**'

The cell began to affect Yvette as soon as they went in. '**I can't explain or understand what happened to me in there,**' she says. '**One moment I felt sick to my stomach and then I just wanted to sob. There were no thoughts in my head, just dreadful sadness.**' She left the room crying as if her heart was breaking and remained inconsolable for some time after.

Yvette cried inconsolably in Derby Gaol
as Karl attempted to comfort her.

'It was embarrassing,' she said later, 'because until then, I'd never cried on camera before. Only at home, in private, with my husband. Before that moment I'd been perfectly happy; in fact, earlier on I'd been singing. I can't explain why I suddenly became so emotional.'

There was definitely something going on in that cell. The cross trigger object moved, orbs were photographed and several people noticed a strong smell of roses – 'As strong as walking into a florist,' says Yvette. Derek believes that what Yvette experienced was a blast of the residual energy of a man who was just about to be taken out and hanged, drawn and quartered. (For more on crisis apparitions, see p. 154.)

Alex Feels Needy at Mary King's Close

This was the first *Most Haunted* shoot that Alex Lysaght came along to, and it affected her very strongly. She explains: '**The story was that a little girl called Annie had been left on her own after all the rest of her family died of the plague that was sweeping Edinburgh at the time. Karl, Tom, Stuart and I went up to do a vigil in the room that had been Annie's. Her spirit has often been heard crying there, so over the years lots of people have sent presents to try and cheer her up. The room is full of stuffed animals, toys and dolls.**

'As we walked in, a tiny teddy bear whizzed past and landed at Tom's feet. We sat down in a semicircle and somehow that teddy made its way to the centre. Every time I looked at it, it had moved … And all of a sudden, I found the whole experience totally overwhelming and

Who made the teddy bear move at Mary King's Close?

I burst into tears. The only thought in my head was that I needed to be hugged. I'm sure I was picking up on the feelings of that poor little girl, Annie, all on her own, missing her family.'

Karl's Headaches

Down in a dark basement, you begin to notice that Karl is clutching his head and frowning some time before he mentions it to the group. He always describes feeling as though his head is '**in a vice**' – and this invariably seems to precede some kind of paranormal activity. Consider the following:

- He got a headache in the Edinburgh Vaults just before 'Mr Boots' touched his face and then the back of his neck with a freezing cold hand.

- He had a headache in the House of Detention just before something scratched his face and then hit him on the head.

- He got a headache in the sealed room at the Manor House Restaurant, in West Bromwich, and at the same time Stuart got pains down the side of his spine to his pelvis and Jon Dibley felt very uncomfortable. Soon after, there was a scratching at the panelling and a banging sound.

- In the cellar at the Station Hotel, in Dudley, Karl felt as though his skull was being crushed, Phil Whyman picked up EMF fluctuations and some spirit lights twinkled, and then Derek told them the spirit had gone and Karl's headache simultaneously disappeared.

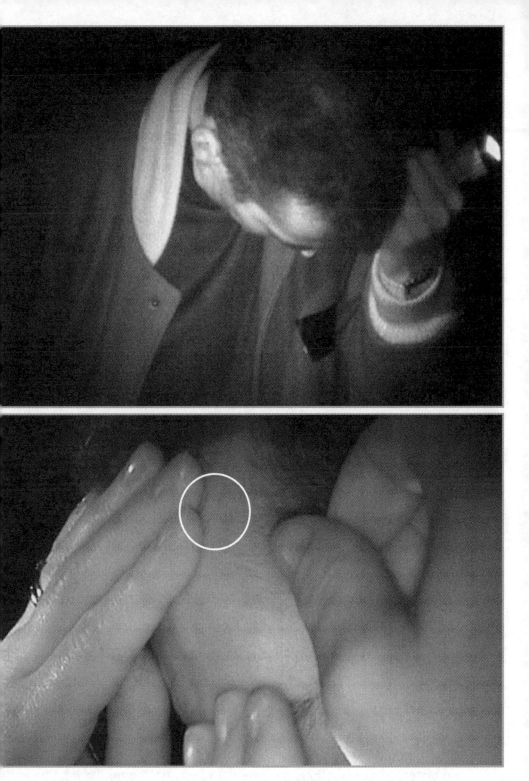

Karl's forehead was scratched in the House of Detention.

And there are many, many more examples of this. The team are learning to pay attention when Karl gets a headache. The man seems to be a walking barometer for paranormal activity!

Rachel's Mood Swings

Here are some of Rachel Philips's experiences: '**Sometimes you walk into a place and sense the atmosphere straight away. At other times you're busy during the day and moods creep up on you gradually … I've had several experiences like this. I'd been in a very happy mood when we arrived at Sandbach Old Hall, then before long I felt like bursting into tears for no reason. In some places I've felt suddenly irritable, then in others I'm drained of energy. In the séance at Annersley Hall, I was sitting next to David Wells and could feel a lady trying to take him over. Fortunately, you can be very open with David so I've discussed these things with him, and he's given me advice about breathing properly and wiggling your toes. Ciaran might say "You're just feeling tired", but I know my own feelings and I recognize depression when I see it.'**

Jon's Terror at Belgrave Hall

Cameraman Jon Dibley (known to his friends as 'Dibs') is one of the most sceptical members of the team and often the first to come up with a rational explanation for odd occurrences. '**Maybe I don't get so disturbed as the others because I'm concentrating on the job I've** got to do. I'm viewing the action through a viewfinder, so maybe that makes me less involved.

'Normally, I barely listen to the stories about the property. Karl will just tell me what I need to know about the place we're filming. I remember on the second shoot I ever went on, at the Station Hotel in Dudley, I felt incredibly sad as soon as I went into one of the bedrooms. I couldn't understand it because I'd been in a good mood beforehand. It was only later that Derek told me I was picking up on the spirit of a young girl who died there.'

There are a few other places where Jon has become suddenly and inexplicably depressed, but nothing that affected him as much as the Celebrity Special with Vic Reeves and Nancy Sorrell at Belgrave Hall, in Leicester. It had been an eventful night all round before they sat down to do a séance in the hall. Derek had picked up on the very dominant, nasty spirit of Edmund Cradock, who built the house in 1709, as well as the gentle Ellis sisters, who were angry with Edmund. Rick Fielding had collapsed, feeling very faint, in the second-floor nursery and Tom's brand-new 12-hour battery had mysteriously been drained. Stuart saw a white figure walking along the wall (see p. 92) and a journalist called Sophie Tweedale also saw a ghostly figure sitting next to Rick.

As soon as the séance began, Derek started breathing heavily, becoming so disturbed that when they tried to bring him forward, he leapt at Stuart, grabbed his throat and wouldn't let go. Could it have been the spirit of Edmund Cradock causing havoc? Derek was still having so much trouble breathing after he evicted the spirit that he had to go outside, and the group continued with the séance on their own.

Here's Jon's description of what happened next: '**Normally in a séance, I'll be standing outside the group filming, or I'll have set up four or five lock-off cameras and while the others are trying to contact spirits, I'll be thinking to myself, "Is that one running? Is it at the best angle?" At Belgrave Hall, I was sitting between Yvette and Cath, with Vic Reeves and his wife opposite. I'd say I was in a very relaxed state of mind. I asked the spirit to make himself known, as we usually do, and suddenly I felt my legs go stiff and a rush of energy go through me, just as if something was trying to control me. I was hurting Cath's hand because in my shock I couldn't stop gripping her.**'

All the team could see was that Jon was shaking and bending double, obviously not himself and barely responding to their queries. Meanwhile, Yvette felt as though her legs were lifting up off the floor and suddenly Karl collapsed, feeling overcome. Both Jon and Karl had to be taken outside to recover in the night air.

DRAINING BATTERIES

Can spirits drain energy from the batteries the team use for night filming? According to Stuart, he can take a fully charged lithium battery that should last 1 hour and 20 minutes and soon after he switches on and starts a walkabout, it's dead and needs to be recharged. This is such a common occurrence that they always travel with truckloads of spare batteries as well as chargers.

From left to right:
Tom, Craig, Yvette, Karl, Vic
Reeves, Nancy Sorrell, with
Derek in the foreground and Jon
Dibley to the right.

VIC REEVES AT BELGRAVE HALL

When Karl got an email from Vic Reeves saying that he loved the show and wanted to be on it, he thought it was a wind-up. 'I didn't reply to that first email so then he phoned, and still I thought someone was having a laugh. Finally I agreed to pop round to their house for a chat and - blow me - it was Vic and his wife, Nancy. I was delighted, and they both helped to make it a very good show.'

Vic (alias Jim Moir) has psychic abilities. He told Yvette that he speaks to the spirit of his grandfather on a regular basis. During the night at Belgrave Hall, he became very emotional at certain points and seemed to be very receptive to atmospheres. In the upstairs nursery, he got the impression that it was too messy and 'someone' wanted to tidy it. During a lone vigil on the stairs, he got a terrible shock. 'I was being quite cocky and then - I dunno - I saw a little red light, heard two creaks and a bang and that's it, I was off.' He fled down the stairs and back to the group like a bat out of hell. After all the turmoil at the séance, Vic felt driven to run up the stairs to the top of the house - 'It was as if I was chasing the spirit away. I was thinking, "Go away, you wanker!"' When the team caught up with him with their cameras, he was sweating and seemed on the verge of tears. It seems Vic had picked up a wide range of emotions from the spirits in Belgrave Hall.

Vic saw a little red light on the staircase.
According to Derek, this could have been a demonic presence.

Jon says: 'I didn't want to go back in that house. I was far too scared. Derek told me I'd been taken over by that very dominant man, the builder of the house, but fortunately it wasn't a full-on possession – just a fleeting visit. I was very lucky. Derek says the spirit chose me because, without him there, I was one of the most susceptible in the group.'

Getting Burned at the Manor House Restaurant

Built in 1290, this property in West Bromwich had gone through several incarnations before it became a restaurant in the 1950s. However, records state that way back in the sixteenth century a fire destroyed the kitchen block. As soon as Derek arrived, he began to get a sickly feeling and said that the heat was getting stronger and flames were engulfing him. He picked up on a pretty little three-to-five-year-old girl he called Emily. (This is strange, because it's the name staff give to the ghostly little girl they've seen there.) Seemingly, Emily had an accident standing too close to the big kitchen fireplace. She toppled over and fell in, and her grandmother Sarah rushed to save her but became engulfed by flames too.

As Yvette was standing listening to the story, she began to feel as though her hand was burning up, from the little finger to the wrist. **'It was as if someone had poured boiling water on my hand. There was a real burning sensation and it took a good half hour to go. It felt the same temperature externally to people who touched it, and didn't look any different, but I found it very painful.'** Derek said that she was walking through the residual energy of the grandmother and the little girl and was bound to take some of it on board, since she was a woman as well.

For an even stranger story of burning flesh, see the next chapter. It's one thing to 'feel' burning but it's quite a bit more scary when the others can actually smell it as well!

Second World War planes are on display in the airfield at RAF East Kirkby.

CHAPTER 12

RAF East Kirkby, Lincolnshire

Imagine going to an exhibition full of the mangled, twisted wreckage of car accidents in which people have died gruesome deaths. Think of the suffering: the limbs sheared off, chests crushed and flesh charred to a cinder. RAF East Kirkby airfield is just like this, except it displays aeroplanes that crashed in the area during the Second World War. All of the tortuous piles of metal on show have taken people's lives and, in many cases, the occupants would have had a few seconds before impact in which they knew they were about to die. If you believe the 'stone tape' theory, that dramatic memories can be recorded in physical surroundings, then what stories would the wreckage at East Kirkby have to replay, and how would it affect the *Most Haunted* team?

The atmosphere or the residual energies in the airfield museum were so strong that Derek had quite extraordinary success in naming the men who had crashed in each plane and telling their tragic stories, often relating what happened during their final moments in the physical body.

- There was Sergeant Arthur Henderson and Sergeant Robert Banks, two gunners who were killed in 1945 after a collision with a

CRISIS APPARITIONS

A crisis apparition manifests itself to the subject's loved ones at moments of extreme crisis, notably when they are dying or know they are about to die. Some of them are seen to gesture at their fatal wounds while others just come to explain what has happened, either in dreams or waking visions. This seems to be one of the most common paranormal experiences we encounter in the physical body. Most of us know someone who has been visited by a vision of a parent, partner or close friend around the time of their death. David describes driving home up the motorway after his sister had called to tell him that his father was dying. 'Suddenly I felt a tapping on my head as I drove and the word "father" came into my head, and I knew that he had gone. He was letting me know.'

Lancaster bomber. When Derek touched their aircraft, he felt the terror and great sorrow of their last moments in the physical body, when they were shouting to each other and knew they were going to die.

- There was Jon Pullam and his friend Dearing, who kept saying through Derek: **'Why are they forgetting me?'** He insists he's not going to leave until he gets answers. He feels resentful that they were **'wrong in the control tower'** and that what happened to him should never have happened.

- There was Canadian pilot Norman Watt, who was refused permission to land on 1 July 1943, even though he was low on fuel, and as a result crashed several miles away. His spirit remains grounded, because he wants an apology, but Derek says he's a good soul who should go into the light.

- In the control tower, Derek picked up Robert Hutchins and Sergeant Robert Hay, who crashed in 1944 when one engine malfunctioned – but Robert Hay survived the crash and lived till 1989. They talked to Derek about checking the engines and being pleased that they were working.

The most extraordinary story that Derek picked up that day concerned a wallet. Suddenly, in the middle of his walkabout, he patted his trousers and said, '**I haven't got my wallet with me.**' Yvette and Phil Whyman grinned at each other in amazement, because they knew there was a story concerning a wallet at the airfield – and they couldn't think of any way Derek could have known about it.

Derek continued: '**He couldn't be where he wanted to be, so he decided he might as well go up. But there's something in his wallet he's concerned about … A paper or document about something he was to collect and if he had done it, he wouldn't have gone down. He loved vehicles, loved cars … He was due to collect a vehicle from the garage on the day he died.**'

Richard Felix explains: '**There was a crashed aircraft that had only recently been dug up, along with the remains of the pilot and a perfectly preserved wallet. Inside that wallet was a piece of paper about a car that was to be picked up from the garage that day.**

Derek, Yvette and Phil examine the papers found
in the wallet of a pilot who crash-landed.

The car wasn't ready after all, so the pilot cancelled his leave and took to the air – and crashed. Now, that wallet was hidden away in a tin in a Nissan hut, not on display in the museum. I didn't know anything about it until we arrived and the owner mentioned it. This incident proved a lot to me about just how good a medium Derek is. I know he couldn't have heard about the wallet, except from the spirit of its owner.'

Even Ciaran was impressed by this: 'Derek came up with some compelling information about the pilot. It's not a high-probability statement, so couldn't have been guessed. I think it's good evidence.'

This piece of paper told them that he should have been picking up his car from the garage on the day he died.

The Night Vigil

The team had a feeling it was going to be an eventful night even before they put the lights out and switched to night-vision cameras. The owner's son, Jonathan, joined them and it wasn't long before he and Karl saw the shadowy figure of a man wearing a cap and pointing towards an old bomber (see p. 94 for the story). Who was he, and what was he trying to tell them?

They split up into groups and separated out to different parts of the hangar. Phil and Rick Fielding soon saw a huge orb just near the bomber the ghost had pointed at. Karl, Yvette and Craig Harman stayed near

Rick Fielding and Craig Harman were utterly petrified during their night vigil in the hangar.

where the shadow had been seen and heard two stones thrown from above hitting a glass cabinet. Rick and Craig later did a vigil on their own in the hangar and were so terrified that they clung to each other for dear life. They didn't have to wait long before they heard tapping and knocking, and then Rick saw something walking past to his right. **'There's some stuff going on here, I'm telling you, boys. My nerves are shot,'** he said. It wasn't long before they got so freaked out they had to leave.

Meanwhile, something very strange was happening to Jonathan. Despite the fact that the outside temperature was below freezing and inside wasn't much warmer, he became overcome with heat and his skin was burning to the touch. Derek tried to calm him down, and when the others came over to see what was happening, they all felt the temperature of his skin. Karl and Yvette decided to take him outside for some fresh air – and within five minutes he felt fine again and his temperature returned to normal.

Next, Karl mentioned to the group that his left arm was getting rather hot. He remembers: **'I didn't know what it was at first, then I thought it was a muscle spasm, but it got worse and worse over the next three or four minutes until it became unbearable. I pulled up my sleeve and there was a stench like burned bacon. It was awful, sweet and sickly.'**

The others all came over to look and smell his arm. **'Oh my God, it stinks!'** exclaimed Yvette. **'Yuck, that *is* burnt,'** said Craig. Tom, Phil and Derek all smelled it straight away. Ciaran comments: **'While there might be some level of group conformity to suggestion, it's notable**

Karl's arm smelled distinctly of burning flesh.

on film that they can all smell it immediately. It's a fantastic, genuine phenomenon.'

According to Derek, the spirit of a man stuck in a burning aircraft was transferring his final experience before he died to Karl's – and to Jonathan's – bodies. He says it's the spirit's way of making a point and getting you to understand what they went through. Isn't that what we all want in this world – understanding and sympathy? It seems it's the same in the next.

Derek explains that spirits will try all kinds of things to make you notice them: **'They produce smells, noises, or they transfer sensations. Here they were thinking, "Let Karl experience this and see what it feels like." Sometimes they want you to understand something, or they're just checking you out or they want attention. The *Most Haunted* team are becoming much more sensitized, so I think we'll be seeing a lot more of this kind of thing.'**

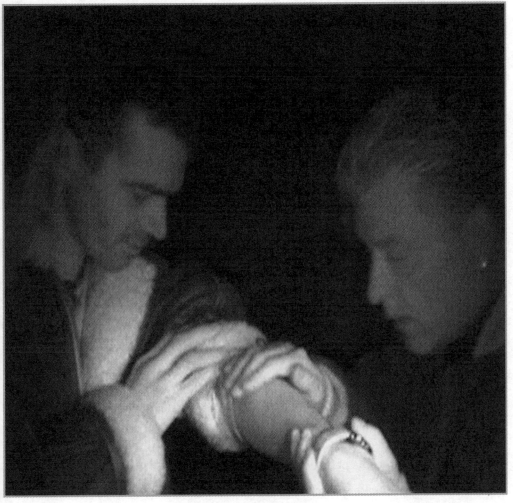

The hairs on his arm appeared to be singed.

THE CONTROL TOWER

The old tower where traffic into and out of the airport was monitored remains a busy place. Since East Kirkby was closed down as an airfield in 1970, locals have reported seeing green lights shining inside the tower at night, even though there was no electricity supply. And the old-fashioned Bakelite telephones have been heard to ring, although none of them are connected. Richard left some books behind at the end of the shoot and had to go back in for them on his own. He says: 'The control tower was known to be very haunted, and I must admit that I was running like a big kid!'

Psychometry

If people can pick up residual energies from buildings, then it makes sense that they can also do it from smaller inanimate objects. Derek, David and Ian Lawman all claim to be able to read the energies in objects, a practice which is known as psychometry.

Derek got some of his amazing results in the hangar at East Kirkby by touching the old relics of planes and other exhibits in the museum. He says: '**I was never drawn to psychometry but I did little bits over the years and was pleasantly surprised at the stuff that came through. Paintings, jewellery and furnishings are best, while fabrics are least energized. I once appeared on *This Morning* and they brought me**

Mangled wreckage on display in the East Kirkby hangar.

two T-shirts and asked me to psychometrize them, but I had to explain they weren't very good for that.'

Ian did some psychometry for *Most Haunted* at the Wellington Hotel in Cornwall. '**Yvette gave me a ring and I couldn't decide if it had belonged to a male or a female, because all I could see was the shape of a hand. Anyway, it turned out that a fisherman had caught a pike and when he opened it up, they found a finger inside with the ring on it. That's why I couldn't visualize the owner!**'

David was put on the spot at the live show in Derby when they asked him to psychometrize three objects in front of the audience. '**I thought, "Thanks a lot, guys!" The first object they gave me was a bayonet and** they asked, "What do you think it was used for?" It was on the tip of my tongue to say, "Erm, killing people?", but then I saw an image that this bayonet had been found in a very strange place, hidden behind a secret wall, and fortunately I was right. Then they gave me a block of wood, like a garden gate, and I could feel a lot of powerful emotion in it. It had been used for hanging, drawing and quartering, and I could feel, see, hear, smell someone on the block having their head removed and being ripped down the middle by a knife. The third object was a key. I couldn't place it historically – all I could see was love, weddings and marriage. It turns out it's the key to a room in the location where people get married. The way to psychometrize is through emotion. There's no point in giving me a coin that has been in and out of so many pockets. Something very personal is best.'

Try picking up a piece of jewellery at an antiques market some time and see if you can visualize the person who used to wear it. You might be surprised at the clarity of image you perceive – alternatively, you might just find the dealer breathing down your neck, trying to make a sale.

CHAPTER 13

Round the Table

The three Fox sisters of New York created a sensation in 1848 when they announced that they were able to communicate with spirits by clapping their hands and listening to hear whether the spirits tapped for '**yes**', '**no**' or a particular letter of the alphabet. They began to demonstrate their skills at public meetings, and the press furore was overwhelming. They held séances at which objects moved, tables levitated and turned, and, despite intensive investigations, no trickery was ever established. Their influence was enormous and the spiritualist church became all the rage in the 1860s and 1870s, although it began to wane thereafter. 'Table-tipping' and 'table-turning' were briefly in vogue but by the early years of the twentieth century, most dismissed them as 'Victorian parlour trickery'.

When they were filming series 5, Yvette and Karl decided to try these old techniques and see what kind of results they got. As far as they are aware, they have never been attempted on television before. You need a circular table, and all the participants sit or stand with their fingers lightly balanced on the edge. You ask the spirits specific questions and, for table-turning, suggest that they turn it clockwise for yes and anticlockwise for no. With table-tipping, you ask them to tilt it in a particular direction for yes and another for no. Place a marble or a candle in the centre and the slightest of movements will be obvious – but check that there are no draughts in the room first.

What does the pragmatic Ciaran think of all this, and does he join in? **'Some researchers think that your level of belief is very important when it comes to things like table-tipping, and although I consider myself open-minded, I don't want my responses to affect the experiment, so I usually stand back and observe rather than join in. At Castle Leslie, in Ireland, the table they were using appeared to levitate twice. I could see it and feel it, but as a scientist the level of proof I need is much higher. Someone could have been lifting it from underneath with their thumbs. When I set a camera on the floor under the table, it didn't levitate any more. Another theory is that the table could move**

FILMING TABLES

The camera angles can be tricky when you have four (or more) participants close together around a smallish table. If the table starts to turn or tip, the team try to have someone who can direct a camera underneath the table to show what's going on from below. Jon Dibley films from above: 'I always film people's hands when we're table-tipping. You know how your fingernails go white if you're pressing on something? I'm trying to show that's not happening. If we cover that aspect visually, it gives more of a balanced argument.'

due to psychokinesis – the power of the mind over matter. If you are focusing hard and visualizing what you want to happen, is it possible that your mind could cause the table to move?' We'll be examining these theories further in this chapter.

Richard Felix has had some notable results when table-tipping. '**At Ordsall Hall** [in Manchester], **there was a young lady called Margaret Radcliffe, a lady-in-waiting to Queen Elizabeth. Her twin brother had died fighting in Ireland and, overcome with grief, she had starved herself to death. When we were table-tipping, I asked if Margaret was there and the table went crazy, rocking all over the place. It turns out she thought she couldn't go to the light because she had committed suicide, so she and her brother were both grounded. Ian Lawman helped them to go over. I got very emotional though. I think I was picking up her sadness, because I was actually crying. It's very strange when a spirit is answering your questions as clearly as she was, by moving the table ...**' Ciaran was present at this session and found the movement of the table '**very impressive**', although he would have liked more scientific controls to be in place before he would rate it as hard evidence of paranormal activity.

At some locations, the table techniques produced some very dramatic results ...

Bodelwyddan Castle, Clwyd

Richard had another remarkable table-tipping experience in this spooky Victorian mansion. '**I was with Karl and Stuart in the cellar at**

Bodelwyddan Castle when a table was thrown at me by the spirit of a murderer. It came right up and hit me. So I would definitely say that table-tipping is an effective means of communication, although you don't always get the answers you were expecting.'

Karl and Yvette then decided to try glass-divination, a technique that simply involves each person resting a finger on a glass in the middle of the table and inviting spirits to move it. Ciaran was observing and David was there to assist, and everyone was impressed by the results.

Karl explains: '**David contacted the spirits of my granddad and Yvette's grandmother. We had a glass on the table and we were asking the spirits questions, saying "move right for yes" or "move left for no", and it was right every time – things David couldn't possibly have known, like my grandmother's first name, how many kids they had, the age when he died. When I checked after, I found that every-thing had been right, down to the smallest details and dates. At one point I took my fingers off the glass and it continued to move and answer the questions.**'

Yvette joins in: '**When my grandmother came through, I sang three tunes and asked her to move the glass on the song that was her favourite, and she did. Then I asked, "Is your husband's name John, Bernie or Eric?", and she moved on the right answer. I was crying, so David asked my grandmother to give me a sign that she was there and the glass moved slowly towards me, then I felt my right hand icy cold, as if a ghostly hand was holding it. The thermal-imaging camera showed everyone's hand was red, except mine was blue. Ciaran found it extraordinary.**'

The Golden Fleece, York

Perhaps one of the most dramatic glass-moving sessions they've ever had was at the Golden Fleece, a pub in York. Scott Mills from Radio 1 had asked to come along that night with some of the team from his radio show, because they were all big fans of *Most Haunted*.

'I don't think they had any idea what they were letting themselves in for,' says Yvette. 'When we put the glass on the table and started asking questions, it began tipping up, hovering, bouncing on the surface, and the Radio 1 guys were cowering in the corner. They're going "Shit! Shit!" and getting very frightened. I caught a couple of

The glass moved dramatically at the Golden Fleece in York.

PUB PICKPOCKET

A few team members felt their back pockets being tugged while they went about their work in the Golden Fleece. It felt as though someone was trying to take their wallet out, but when they looked no one was there. This had been reported by other visitors to the Golden Fleece, and David picked up the spirit of a little boy called Christian, who admitted that he is a pickpocket. Jon Gilbert, who was doing the sound that night, had a more alarming experience. 'My penknife opened up inside my pocket and cut my fingers,' he says. 'I never put the blade away like that, so something must have made it open. All the lads felt their wallets being touched or lifted, or things tugging on their pockets.'

light anomalies round them. That's when I said to the spirit, "If you want us to leave, give us a sign", and I heard these three sniggers – "Huh, huh, huh" – and burst into tears … David got in touch with the spirit and told us that it was a highwayman called Robert. He and his lover had killed three women for money and they didn't want us to be there.'

Stuart remembers the scene well: 'The glass was whizzing round furiously, really viciously. Karl took his fingers off so it was just Yvette and Cath, but it was still going strong and the footage doesn't show any pressure on their fingernails. I think the Radio 1 chaps didn't really believe anything would happen when they came along, but they left in quite a different frame of mind.'

They weren't the only ones to get such definite responses in that room. Earlier, Alex Lysaght, Yvette, Karl and Rachel Philips had tried glass-moving, supervised by Ciaran, while the others weren't around. Alex recalls: **'The glass started spinning wildly. It went to fly off the table two or three times. Someone was definitely trying to tell us something!'**

Maes Artro, Gwynedd

There have been sightings of more than 30 different ghosts at this former RAF base in north-west Wales. With so many spirits present and with such a wide area to explore, the team decided to use 'round table' techniques to try to contact the ones who were willing to communicate.

They began with a séance in the Officers' Mess, where Derek first of all contacted Squadron Leader Ian Moran, but soon several other spirits were crowding in, trying to say their piece. There were a number of men who had died in accidents, both during the war and after. Brian Shepherd was sketching in the corner, and he became a bit overwhelmed at one point. **'Sometimes it's hard to shake off when you perceive something so strongly,'** he says. **'There were several people coming through and I was getting confused. There was a wing commander who oversees the whole area, and he had died more recently and come back to join his old colleagues who died in the war, because that was where his spirit wanted to be. I felt a real camaraderie between them all, but**

Brian sketching at Maes Artro.

also a sadness that so many people had died in one place. I couldn't get free of some of the spirits and Derek picked up that I was having problems and helped me out, saying "Let it go, let it go".'

Both Derek and Brian felt their faces and hands burning up when they communicated with Flight Lieutenant Geoffrey Paige. '**Take it off! His face is terrible!**' Derek yelled, clutching at his own face. Richard found out that there was a man of that name who had been very badly burned in an air accident in 1943, and had gone through extensive plastic surgery afterwards, but didn't die until 1980. He suggested that Derek and Brian were picking up the residual energies of a crisis apparition created by Flight Lieutenant Paige at the time of the accident and stored in the stones of the Maes Artro complex.

Next, the team tried a glass-moving experiment in the old morgue. Yvette, Cath, Derek and floor manager Sally Matthews sat round the table while Ciaran supervised the group from outside the circle. First of all the glass began to vibrate. Ciaran kept asking people to take their fingers off the glass at random, so he could be sure that no one person was responsible for the movement. Suddenly, Yvette felt a freezing cold blast of air across her legs – **'Like an ice-cold whirlwind,'** she says. Sally announced she could smell tobacco smoke, although there was no one smoking in the building. The glass whizzed across the table and stopped in front of Yvette, and she sat, scared and shivering, as it hovered there. Ciaran was surprised to note that the room temperature had suddenly dropped by 2°C.

Derek picked up a spirit called Bingo Brown, an air vice-marshal who said he was foreign. (Richard later confirmed that Bingo Brown was South African.) The glass moved towards Sally next and she felt the icy gust on her legs and hands, and then it moved on to Cath. **'I got a bad headache and felt very sick and faint,'** she recalls. **'Derek said I was picking up on the atmosphere around me, and helped to calm me down.'** Suddenly, the glass began to whizz in super-fast circles. **'It was spinning round and round so fast I was completely freaked out,'** says Yvette.

This was a live event, so the audience and various experts were watching what was happening on a big screen. Sceptic Louie Sava believed that the movement of the glass was caused by unconscious micro-muscular movements. David said that **'spirit channels through** their bodies' were causing the movement. The arguments aren't too far apart, except that Louie thinks that the initial impetus comes from the subconscious mind of a living person whereas David thinks it comes from the will of a spirit person. David believes the team are getting more and more results from spirit communication techniques with every show. **'Their awareness is heightening all the time,'** he says. **'Yvette's emotional responses in particular are a clear indication of this.'**

Next, they decided to try table-tipping back in the Officers' Mess. Yvette, Derek, Cath and Karl stood around the table with their fingers lightly resting on the top. Ciaran patrolled round the perimeter of the group, asking them to raise their fingers in sequence and at random. A man named MacPhearson came through, whom Derek had earlier identified as being responsible for some strange shuffling noises in that room. The table began to turn as Yvette asked the questions.

'Are you a married man?' she asked, and the table turned for yes. **'Do you have children? One? Two? Three?'** The table turned on three. **'Is your wife with you now?'** The answer was a definite yes. **'Do you like dancing?'** Yvette asked, and he replied yes; then she cheekily asked, **'Or did you like to look at the other ladies?'** Yvette remembers what happened next: **'At that point, the table came for me and smacked right across the top of my thigh. In the morning I had a huge long bruise where it had rammed me.'**

Back in the studio, they debated exactly what had made that table move. Ciaran considered the subconscious micro-muscular movement theory: **'Faraday was looking into this back in 1852 and it's still an open book … In this case, though, you could have seen instantly if** anyone was pushing the table, because I had placed a cloth on top and it would have ruched up with the pressure of their fingers.'

Karl says: 'We were checking up on each other while the table was moving. If Derek had been pushing, I would have felt it, and he would have felt it if I was.' At one point, all four of them had just one finger on the table, yet it was still tipping and turning around in answer to their questions, as if responding to pressure from quite another source entirely.

CRYSTALS

David has given Yvette an amethyst pendant to help her open up and become more psychically in tune. 'Amethyst is an all-rounder among crystals,' he explains. 'I gave all the rest of the crew obsidian, a black crystal which is very earthing and will help them keep their feet on the ground as they develop.' When the team went to Tynedale Farm, in Clitheroe, Yvette forgot her crystal, so Karl gave her his and halfway through the séance he had a disturbing experience. 'I felt detached and disdainful of everyone. I said, "You're all pathetic", and I remember I wanted to strangle Cath. Basically I had no control over what I was saying.' David thinks that one of the Pendle Witches might have got inside Karl briefly, but he was fine as soon as he went outside. David says: 'In future I should carry a big box of spare crystals to protect anyone who forgets theirs.'

Could it have been psychokinesis that made the glass or the table move in all these cases? Did the participants subconsciously create the result they were hoping for with the power of their minds? Or were the spirits of RAF officers channelling energy through their fingers in order to communicate with them? One thing is for sure: in later series, when the team are prepared to challenge spirits they encounter, they get even more dramatic results … as you'll see in the next chapter.

CHAPTER 14

Owlpen Manor, Gloucestershire

By the fourth series of *Most Haunted*, the team were getting braver. Rather than sitting around all night waiting to see if anything would happen, they were starting to challenge potential spirits and even provoke them to action. It doesn't mean they were any less scared – **'I get more scared every time,'** admits Stuart. Rather, they're keen to progress and amass more and more footage of activity that could ostensibly be paranormal. And they were certainly going to get plenty to chew on at Owlpen Manor.

It would all be very well provoking ghosts if they were nice, polite, well-brought-up ones like Margaret of Anjou, who is said to visit Owlpen regularly. She was Queen of England after her marriage to Henry VI in 1445, but they had a problem: the Duke of York wanted to oust them from the throne, and in 1455, he began the Wars of the Roses to try to secure it for himself. Poor Margaret's sole aim in life was to ensure the succession of her son, Edward, but her heart was broken after he was killed at the Battle of Tewkesbury in 1471. She was imprisoned for five years before being allowed to return to her French homeland, penniless.

Derek began to describe Margaret of Anjou soon after he arrived at Owlpen Manor. '**She's a very gracious lady, who dresses in many different colours, she has so many** [costumes] **... But there's a tinge of sadness about her, from a tragedy ... a young male who meant so much to her was taken away and killed.**' Derek was able to sense that she has been reunited with her son in the spirit world and is thrilled to be with him again.

Very early in the evening, both Yvette and Derek were picking up a more disturbing sensation in the corridor outside the Queen's Bedroom. Yvette had already said she didn't like that particular corridor when suddenly she began to experience excruciating pain in her lower back. '**I know every woman has had back pain at some time,**' she says, '**but this was a horrible, severe, aching pain. I'd been absolutely fine earlier in the day. I don't know what it was. Maybe I'd been standing in the wrong position for a wee while.**' But according to Derek, the spirit in the corridor was responsible for her pain. '**He's zapping your energy through your spine. I've had that myself, and it's not nice.**' It seemed to come and go over the next few hours and was particularly painful in certain parts of the manor.

Derek named the negative spirit as Daniel and explained that he's the kind of person who would appear jovial on the outside, greeting visitors with great warmth and personality, but underneath is manipulative, cajoling and capable of evil practices. He told Yvette, '**He's the type of person that if he was here, he would do horrible, unspeakable things to you. His intent is pure evil.**' In the Attic Room, Derek picked up clashes between Daniel and a man called Daunt (the Daunts were owners of Owlpen from 1462 to 1803). '**The negative soul hates**

Owlpen Manor: a medieval house which has been extended over the centuries.

Yvette films her opening pieces to camera.

Daunt, and Daunt is not as powerful as him, but he still stands up to him.'

It soon became very apparent to the team that someone – or something – did not want them to be in that Attic Room. What was to follow was one of the clearest cases of poltergeist activity that the team have ever experienced. And this time they caught it on camera.

The Books

Ian Lawman accompanied Karl, Yvette, Stuart, Jon Dibley and the owner's dog, who is deaf, up to the Attic Room, where the ghost of the 7th Thomas Daunt, a wizard and alchemist, had been seen. Ian decided to challenge the spirit he sensed there, in order to provoke a reaction. He explains: **'It's a scary technique but I always stand up to spirits. Nine times out of ten, they'll back down – and if we have a fight, they'll tire of it first.'**

He said, **'Spirit within this room, please give us a sign. We're not going to move out of this room until you make a noise.'** There was a sound of movement, a creaking of boards, and Ian reported that the spirit was getting angry. **'You're not going to move us away**

The dog kept barking and growling into one corner of the attic.

They examine the fallen books by torchlight.

with that. That's rubbish – give us something better.' There was a further tapping and creaking, and the dog squealed, then suddenly Karl yelled. A book from the tightly packed bookshelves the room was lined with had somehow hit him on the back of the head. No one else was nearby.

'It was as though something was teasing us,' remembers Karl.

'My nerves were in tatters,' Yvette says. 'There was definitely something in the room with us. We all felt something, even the dog.'

There were more noises, then a long, bright light anomaly, like the glowing filament inside a light bulb, floated past the door. At this stage, the team decided to call Derek up to the Attic Room to see if he could help them get in touch with the spirit, and that's when books really started to fly from the shelves.

At first they thought there might be some significance in the choice of titles:

- The one that hit Karl on the back of the head was *Repair of Ancient Buildings*, by A. R. Powys. Was this a clue? Did the spirit want something repaired?

- Then, out of the corner of his eye, Jon saw one tumble from a shelf – *The Ten Principal Upanishads*, edited by W. B. Yeats. The *Upanishads* are sacred books, written in Sanskrit between about 400 and 200 BC, containing the principles of Hinduism. The page it fell open at had some disturbing hand-drawn images of demonic faces glaring up at them. '**It was really weird,**' says Yvette. '**We turned round and found a book on the bed open to all these horrible pictures.**'

- Next, Jon was hit hard on the leg by *The Forest Primeval*, a collection of poems about ancient forests from the first age of man. '**If that hit someone on the face, it would really hurt,**' he exclaimed, rubbing his leg.

- The owner later showed them a book on heraldry that he had found on the floor, with several pages torn out. Who could have torn it, and why? Was there a message in there?

Two more books followed in quick succession and the team decided it was probably just a random selection rather than deliberate choices,

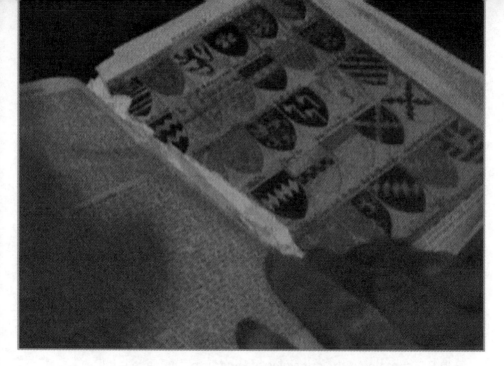

Several pages had been torn from the heraldry book found on the attic floor.

but they hurried to get out before someone was hit on the head and seriously hurt.

What was happening in there? Parapsychologist Matthew Smith outlined the options: **'The footage doesn't entirely rule out the possibility that someone threw those books, but all the crew members maintain they didn't ... They could have been teetering on the shelves and fallen off on their own, but when you look you can see they are very tightly packed. My conclusion is that this is definitely worth further investigation.'**

Karl comments: **'If it was one of the crew doing it, they would have had to sneak in without anyone seeing and hide from four cameras in the room. It would have been pretty elaborate for someone to do that, so it mystifies me. Jon's a sensible guy so when something happens that he can't explain, it really convinces me.'**

Stuart agrees: 'Jon just doesn't lie. He's a straightforward guy. I think it was definitely paranormal. There was someone trying to tell us something.'

Yvette says: 'It frightened me when the dog was barking for no particular reason, walking into the corner of the room and growling. It was very strange.'

Ian firmly believes that the spirit was trying to get a message across to them. 'We'd had a good look round before filming started and the books weren't anywhere near the edge of the shelves. Spirits can give messages through objects. I think this spirit was saying to us, "I am an evil person."'

MAY I INTRODUCE MYSELF?

There was another flying book at Arreton Manor, on the Isle of Wight. That one was called *Ghosts of the Isle of Wight*. Could it have been the ghostly equivalent of a calling card?

The Séance

To finish off the night's filming, the team decided to hold a séance with both Derek and Ian in the circle to help protect them if the nasty spirit came to join them. Sure enough, after they'd waited for half an hour or so, Derek began to shake. He was hissing and wheezing, breathing heavily, even growling like a dog. Ian had to calm everyone down,

Derek and Yvette go head to head during the séance.

because some of the newer team members had never seen Derek like this before. **'They're using Derek as a channel,'** he explained. **'It's OK, friend, come and talk.'**

'Who are you?' Yvette asked. **'Try and communicate.'** Derek leaped to his feet and charged towards her, shouting **'Leave me!'** in an odd, sinister voice.

Tor O'Neill, who was sitting next to Yvette, says: **'She was squeezing my hand so hard she actually bent my ring.'**

'Something in me snapped,' Yvette said later. 'It was peculiar. I lost my temper and thought, "No, you don't scare me. Shut up, sit down!"'

For 30 seconds, she and Derek yelled at each other at the tops of their voices, their faces only inches apart. Karl explains: 'We've got to the point with possessions where we've done that and we have to push it further. Is he going to levitate? Is his head going to spin round? If there's a spirit entity in there, let's have some proof. So the next step is to try and antagonize whatever it is. Derek's a very strong man and he can be very scary when he's in a state like this. When Yvette said, "No, I'm not afraid of you", whatever it was seemed upset by that. But we need proof that things are paranormal, so we have to push that bit further.'

Yvette agrees with him, but adds: 'I was getting worried about the number of violent possessions Derek has had, where he was aggressive to the crew. He's thrown a lamp at me, strangled Stuart, put his hands round Phil Whyman's throat and scared the living hell out of all of us … Don't think I wasn't secretly scared to death [at Owlpen]. I surprised myself when I stood up to someone possessed by a so-called evil entity.'

Ian led Derek away from the circle and began to bring him round. 'He was becoming very, very weak and struggling to come out. It's easier when you have another medium to help. Derek seems to do more channelling in later series than he used to, but it's all part of his way forward.'

Derek comments: 'I'm not a violent man, but the energy of the spirit I'm channelling can be, as it was at Owlpen. I have the privilege of not recalling these events afterwards. I've got family, grandchildren, dogs and cats, and I don't want replays of these things in my head. I work for the spirit and will continue to do so, but I need ordinary time as well.'

Derek hasn't even watched all the shows yet, although he keeps a library of them and occasionally puts one on months later. 'I'm often extremely surprised by what I see, because I usually have no memory of what happened on locations after the filming is over.' He has never watched the events that took place at Owlpen Manor.

CHAPTER 15

Confronting Evil

How can you explain evil if you believe in God? Theologians and philosophers have argued over the 'problem' of evil since time immemorial. If the universe is governed by some kind of supreme being who is both good and omnipotent, then why doesn't he (or she) prevent evil? Either he can and chooses not to, therefore he is not wholly 'good'; or he can't prevent it, in which case he's not all powerful. Or is there another explanation?

As a spiritualist, Derek believes in God, although he is not tied to the tenets of any one particular faith, believing they all have good in them. Spiritualists think that when we leave the physical body we go to one of seven realms on the other side. Derek explains: **'The truth about reincarnation is that we're sent back here to gain perfection or at least travel towards it. In some lifetimes we'll have difficult experiences, we'll have good health or bad health, be rich or poor; and as our spirits progress, we'll move up from the lower realms until eventually, in the seventh realm, we don't have to come back to the physical body any more because our souls are at total peace, with wisdom and contentment.'**

The problem is that spirits who remain grounded on earth tend to be the ones who have been so evil in this lifetime that they are terrified to go over, because they know they'll go to the very lowest realms. Another difficulty the *Most Haunted* team have faced is that there are evil energy forces that don't come from the realms of earth. Derek explains: **'A diva is a living energy, a soul who's broken away from the light and fallen from grace. They are not good souls, they're the negative side of angelic.'**

David doesn't believe in extreme evil. **'In everything there is a spark of light,'** he says, **'but when you are dealing with emotionally**

Derek was very distressed by the evil he encountered in the House of Detention.

disturbed, self-obsessed, angry spirits, they are as hard to deal with as they would be in life.'

Are the team ever in genuine danger from these spirits? When Karl has been shoved or scratched, he says: **'I'd think, "OK, if that's the worst you can do, bring it on!"'** But he could have incurred a serious injury when he was pushed while climbing the ladder at Brannigan's Nightclub. Any of the team could be at risk if they were pushed at the top of a flight of stairs.

It's hard for spirits to sustain enough energy to cause real harm in the physical world, but in this chapter we're going to look at two locations where evil spirits did harm members of the *Most Haunted* team – and in both cases, it took them some time to recover afterwards.

The House of Detention, London

Even before they arrived at this underground prison in Clerkenwell, in London, the team knew it was going to be a tough location. Karl says: **'I'd warned them it wasn't going to be idyllic, so they didn't have to come if they didn't want to.'**

The prison was built at the beginning of the seventeenth century to hold prisoners until they were moved to their final destination – either Newgate, the colonies or the gallows. Around 10,000 prisoners a year were held there, including pickpockets, highwaymen, prostitutes and their children, and some much nastier criminals as well. Many strange noises had been heard, figures had been seen in corridors and through a window, and there was a huge door that mysteriously swung shut by itself every night. More ominously, every other paranormal investigation team that had ever been there had left within a few hours, scared out of their wits.

Jon Dibley describes their first impressions: '**It was very damp, very cold and very oppressive. Moisture in the air kept steaming up the camera lenses and I had to dry them out. It was also very dirty, and a health-and-safety nightmare with huge holes in the floor, which are not great for me when I'm walking backwards to film. A few times, I lost my footing and the camera jerked up.**'

Karl says it's the most depressing place he's ever filmed: '**You're underground, there's the smell of damp, it's freezing cold, the numbers of the cells are on the walls and you know what's gone on down there in the past. It's very sad, not a nice place.**'

The others agreed. Stuart remembers: '**It was nasty. As soon as you walked in, you could hear groans and chains – not physically, but mentally.**' Cath says: '**It was awful, very damp – the worst one, for me. I was very poorly after that shoot. I had a horrible cold that I couldn't get rid of for ages.**' And Yvette had an unwelcome side effect from the dank atmosphere. Her trademark long black leather coat went mouldy from the damp and had to be thrown out.

As soon as Derek arrived, he picked up a despicable spirit and began to experience loads of horrific images flashing into his mind. The first active spirit he described was Jack Sheppard, a notorious highwayman and housebreaker who lived from 1702 to 1724. He had been a celebrity in his day, renowned for daring jail breaks, including one from the House of Detention, but he was finally caught and hanged by the authorities.

Derek also picked up Jack's lover, a prostitute known as Edgeworth Bess, and her little girl, who had been imprisoned there with her, plus Jack's brother, Thomas, who was later transported to the colonies for stealing. **'It's the young girls who were plying their trade, they had the worst time,'** Derek explained, and shuddered.

The team proceeded to a part of the jail known as 'S Wing', and Derek became visibly distressed at the images he was witnessing. **'There's an evil essence of presence … I see people being brought down to the floor, limbs chopped off, and I want to retch. These souls were like pieces of meat to this individual, who did things for his own enjoyment. He was not a jailor but a prisoner who was in a position of trust. He's sordid, sexual, and he performs rape on rape on rape.'** Derek described to the team a man's stomach being torn out of his body, women cut to ribbons, noses split open with a grooved knife and some horrific sexual acts that had been performed on children. Much of what he told them was too graphic and disturbing to be broadcast.

The spirit was taunting Derek, looking for a chance to get inside his aura, but Derek refused to let it in. He described some foul sexual acts the spirit was threatening to perform on Yvette. She says: **'I was furious. I thought, "Come on, then!"'** Next, the spirit began threatening the female crew members and Derek groaned, **'Oh, we've got trouble here, Yvette.'**

Derek's energies were being drained faster than he could replenish them. He had to break off filming a couple of times and go outside for a breather, because something strange was happening to him that he hadn't experienced before. **'I couldn't hear Sam. Somehow they learned to block Sam out, the first time it had ever happened. Even when**

WHAT WILL BECOME OF THE HOUSE?

The owner of the House of Detention, Darren Gowes, had been considering converting the premises into a nightclub but Karl thinks that would be disastrous. 'Building work can bring spirits out, it disturbs them.' However, since the *Most Haunted* programme aired, Darren has been able to charge serious money to parties of 'ghost-hunters' wanting to challenge themselves by doing vigils in there. In Karl's opinion, it should be turned into a museum. There's too much history there to do anything else. Can you imagine what Michael might try with revellers at a disco? It doesn't bear thinking about.

I went outside, the negative energies were following me, feeding off me … Being without Sam, it felt like going down a blind alley. It made me feel very isolated, very alone.'

There were a number of spirits at different levels but Derek became convinced that the truly evil one was Michael, an Irish terrorist, who had blown up the prison in 1867 in an effort to free two Irish prisoners held there. Fifteen died in the explosion.

It wasn't just Derek who was having a terrifying experience. Craig Harman twice heard shuffling footsteps nearby when there was no one there, then felt hands around his throat, choking him. **'It was serious,'** he said. **'I felt all light-headed.'** Rick Fielding thought he heard a child in the exact place where Craig had heard the footsteps. Then Karl was hit on the back of the head by something and felt a razor scratch across his forehead; the camera showed a thin red line, about 4 cm long, appearing on his skin. Could it have been an insect flying past in the dark, as Ciaran later suggested? Or was Michael able to scratch him from the spirit world?

Guarding the Girls

Throughout the night, Derek was most concerned for the safety of the girls and he implored Stuart to stay with them at all times, even if he had to lie across them! 'You're their gatekeeper,' he said.

'I knew it was serious,' Stuart recalls, 'because Derek had never asked me to do that before.' He was sitting in the crew room with Cath, Suzanne Vinton and Wendy James while the others were all at the other side of the building. As we've seen before, there's a time code on the camcorders so that the team can check what each person was doing at any given time. At 2.20 a.m., Derek, Yvette and Phil Whyman were in the Wash Room when Derek said: 'Michael is not going to let you out of here peacefully.' Then he became alarmed and blew air out of his mouth twice, before saying 'He's got the girls. Right now the temperature is going completely flat and cold around the girls. Shouldn't we go there?'

Phil tried to call the girls on the walkie-talkie but there was no reply, so they hurried up there and, sure enough, Stuart and the girls were complaining of the cold. But what's odd is that when they played back the time-coded camcorder tape, it was at exactly 2.20 a.m. that Suzanne

Stuart and the girls at the House of Detention.

said, **'I'm freezing. Absolutely freezing'**, and Stuart said, **'I know. It's got really cold in here.'** The others agreed, and they blew in the air, creating clouds of vapour just as Derek had visualized them doing.

Coincidence? It was a very cold place after all. But the synchronicity of both Derek and Suzanne talking about the cold at 2.20 a.m. on different sides of the building was uncanny.

Just before the temperature dropped, Stuart and the girls had heard footsteps in the corridor. Stuart says: **'I was sure it was Derek because he's the only one who wears shoes. The rest of us are in trainers with** rubber soles, but he has proper shoes.' Anyway, it wasn't Derek. There was no one outside that room at 2.19 a.m. and Derek was still over in the Wash Room. But could it have been the spirit of Irish Michael?

Cath says: '**I can't explain how scared we felt when we heard strong footsteps and thought someone was coming back for us but there was no one there. I was also really scared for Derek that night. He's such a gentleman but he wasn't himself when it all happened. I'd never seen him like that before.**'

Yvette agrees: '**It was such a strong spirit that it frightened us all. When you see anyone as distressed as Derek was, it upsets you**

Yvette would never go back to the House of Detention.

and affects the crew. It took twice as long to film because Derek was so upset, then it upset the girls, and it had a knock-on effect like dominos. I wouldn't ever go back there.'

Karl is typically understated: 'There was definitely something in there. You could see it and hear it.' Would he go back again? 'Sure,' he replies, without hesitation.

The Ancient Ram Inn, Gloucestershire

All the team got a bad feeling soon after they arrived at this thirteenth-century inn in Gloucestershire, which is now the home of a man named John Humphries. 'It's decrepit,' Alex explained. 'It's been condemned. The owner needs to replace the roof but he can't afford it, and there are no fire exits or anything.'

There's a pervasive smell of damp, uneven floors and an open grave in one room. This might partly explain the gloomy feelings that descended on the crew; added to that, there were stories of witchcraft, murder and bodies under the floor. Richard Felix explains: 'There are a lot of earth energies, as the inn was built over an ancient spring at the crossroads of two ley lines.' (For more on ley lines, see p. 230.) Brian Shepherd says: 'That place is steeped in history – Stonehenge is nearby – and witchcraft took place there, so when we walked in you could feel things coming at you right, left and centre.' Cath saw a dark shadow moving in one of the rooms while they were still setting up, in daylight.

As soon as Derek arrived, he picked up on malignant, grounded spirits – as many as six or seven of them. **'I'm getting someone who wants to slash and cut … he is the true essence of evil. He did terrible, terrible things.'** Derek warned them: **'We have to be more careful here than on any other investigation … These are the most cunning, crafty spirits ever and they will feed on our energies. Take care where you are putting your feet, watch out on stairs and don't go off on your own.'** He emphasized that no one should be alone there at any time, for whatever reason.

Among the malevolent spirits, Derek identifed a woman who practised witchcraft round about 1284 and named her as Elspeth Grant. He told the team that she haunts the premises along with her evil cat. **'She is 5 foot, 3 inches, with long, unkempt hair and a masculine face – and she wants to harm us.'** Meanwhile, quite independently, Brian Shepherd was sketching what he could see, and he came up with a picture of a very aggressive-looking cat and then an image of a woman with long straggly hair that seemed to fit Derek's description to a tee. Brian showed his drawings to the owner, who remarked that the woman looked similar to his daughter when she was younger. Could the woman have been an ancestor of his?

Alex, Rachel and Yvette tried using a ouija board to get in touch with the spirits in the house, while Ciaran looked on. The glass started moving from letter to letter, but they couldn't make sense of the answers they were being given. Rachel remembers: **'They were funny letters – lots of Vs, Xs and Ws. It was only later when we got back to the office and I checked on the internet that I found a description of what happened when another group of paranormal investigators did a**

Brian Shepherd's drawing of the woman Derek identified as Elspeth Grant.

Brian's drawing of the cat.

ouija board there. Believe it or not, they came up with the exact same letters as we did.' Maybe an expert in witchcraft should have a look at them to see if there's a message in there.

Yvette was feeling increasingly uncomfortable. 'I'm hating every minute of this. It's a horrible, horrible, horrible place.' Up in the attic, she felt dizzy and disorientated. Stuart got pains in the front of his head, and everyone felt cold spots in different rooms. In the Bishop's Room, on the first floor, Karl was hit on the back of the head (again!). A spirit kept trying to possess Derek and repeating the message 'Go to the barn. Go to the barn'. And so, with trepidation, they did.

The Barn

Derek, Karl, Stuart and Jon made their way to the old barn as the spirit had instructed, and things began to kick off as soon as they arrived. Karl got one of his headaches. '**It feels like I've got something pounding inside my head and a weight on my shoulders,**' he said. Jon felt very strongly that there was someone in the room with them. Stuart saw a red light travelling from left to right just behind Karl, and Derek told them that the colour red signifies a demonic presence.

Stuart got the feeling he could almost see something in one corner of the room. He walked over there, with Derek close behind him, and next thing they knew he was on the floor, screaming in pure terror. Here's his description of what happened: '**I saw a red light, like a red laser pen, and then I became aware of a black shape moving. I turned to Derek and told him I sensed something there but I don't remember his reply because something ran at me and pushed me down. It punched me in the chest, twice, then it's kicking my stomach. I felt the pain and started screaming and crying, trying to cover myself up, but whatever it was was still getting through to me. I can remember Derek saying "Leave him alone" and rubbing my chest, but I told him to stop because it hurt when he did that. My foot was trapped because I'd twisted my ankle when I fell and one of my shoes came off. I crawled out of there on my hands and knees because I was still trying to get my breath back. I couldn't stand up.**'

That wasn't the end of his terrifying experience, though. Just outside the barn, Stuart was sitting on a bench with Rachel, trying to gather his thoughts to record his 'diary cam' description of events, when suddenly he was punched hard on the shoulder by an unseen hand. Rachel recalls: '**We were setting up the diary cam, just Stuart and me there, when he was whacked on the shoulder. I think he must have been goading those spirits. When I arrived, the owner told me to say hello to them and they wouldn't harm me. I don't think Stuart had said hello.**'

According to Ciaran, Stuart was showing symptoms of shock after his experience. He has studied the footage over and over again, watching Stuart's body moving as if under the impact of invisible blows. '**We have to take his testimony that he believed it was happening, but it is rare to capture that kind of interaction. Could it have been a fit? No form of epilepsy would match that. It's frustrating that there wasn't a camera on the other side as he fell, because Derek is in the way.**'

Stuart has never been able to watch the footage because he was so severely traumatized by events there. '**I had big problems after that – sleeping problems and mental problems. I was physically and mentally drained and couldn't sleep at all for three or four nights. I talked to Karl about it mostly, and there was one point when I told him that was it, I couldn't go on any more** [working on *Most Haunted*].'

Karl says: '**Stuart is a dear, dear friend of mine as well as a respected co-worker. It's very difficult when you see a friend in that situation. You think, "Do it to me, not him." He's like a brother. When I saw him that upset, I thought, "Hang on, is this worth it?" He slept at the office afterwards because he was too scared to go home. Then when he said he didn't know if he could continue, I said I would back him whatever he decided, but I hoped he would stay.**'

Just what was it that attacked Stuart in the barn at the Ancient Ram Inn? It wasn't an isolated incident, because the owner has been attacked and thrown across the room at exactly the same point. Two decades ago, the Reverend John Yates, Bishop of Gloucester, tried to exorcize the inn but his attempt failed. Whatever demonic creatures haunt these walls, they seem to have a firm hold.

INCUBI

It is said that there is an incubus among the spirits haunting the Ancient Ram Inn. This is a demon that masquerades as a man in order to get into bed with women and sexually molest them. It can even impregnate them with sperm collected from men in their sleep. The female equivalent, a succubus, is a demon masquerading as a voluptuous woman, who molests men. The owner of the inn reports that he is often woken from his sleep by ghostly hands and on one occasion they actually pulled him out of bed. Why does he stay there? Who knows!

CHAPTER 16

The Nature of Fear

Fear causes a physiological change in most animals, known as the 'fight or flight' response. Watch a cat when it hears a strange noise: it tenses, poised, deciding whether to flee or attack, and the hairs on its back stand on end as it assesses the danger. Adrenalin is released from the adrenal glands, causing the heart rate to go up, thus pumping extra blood to the muscles so that the cat will be able to run its fastest, if necessary. Its pupils also dilate so it can see more clearly.

The same 'fight or flight' response takes place in human beings. In fact, some people develop a taste for the sensation of an adrenalin rush – those who pursue extreme sports, for example. Maybe there is an element of this for the *Most Haunted* team when they enter yet another supposedly haunted property for a 24-hour vigil.

Karl agrees: **'Yes, it's addictive. You want to be more scared tomorrow. If you've been on your own in an attic, you want to be on your own in a dungeon, and if you've been in a graveyard, you think, "Hah! I'll try a morgue next time …" We were a bag of nerves when we first started, but we've progressed so that now, if we have to, say,** lie in a coffin with a dead body, we think, "Well, I won't do that today, but I might do it tomorrow."'

Yvette says: '*Most Haunted* is like a rollercoaster ride. You get on at the beginning not knowing what's going to happen, then you go through the night being absolutely petrified, but when you come off, you think, "Oh my God, I can't wait to go on again!"'

Quite a few of the team admit that they watched horror films in their younger years. Stuart used to stay up late watching Hammer House of Horror films at a very early age, and Cath was also a fan. She says: 'I used to scare myself silly watching horror films, and I went to bed with a cross after, but I obviously like being scared.'

Yvette has become much braver as the series progress.

Of course, in all the best horror films, the scariest moment is not when the vampire has its teeth in the maiden's throat or the psychopath is smashing someone's head on a car roof. It's the minutes before that, when the viewers can see there's a good chance of it happening and are imagining the worst for themselves. As Alfred Hitchcock said in an interview, '**There's no terror in a bang, only in the anticipation of it.**'

Yvette explains: '**People don't like the full blow in the face, they like it slightly out of shot, because what your imagination can come up with is worse than what they show on screen. On our show, the scariest moments are when you're in a room on your own, where you've been told certain things have happened, and you're waiting to see what transpires while your imagination works overtime.**'

Jon Dibley says: '**Ultimately, what I'm scared of is the unknown. When it's dark and unfamiliar, it's always disconcerting. Add to that the fact that someone has died or was murdered in the room you're standing in, and that makes it a lot more terrifying.**'

Karl agrees: '**Yeah, it's fear of the unknown. If there was a human being there, you could reason with them, talk to them, or at the last resort fight them. But if there's nothing there, it's horrible. You don't understand it, and your anticipation is far worse. I mean, is a skeleton going to leap out, or what?**'

But Stuart says: '**I love not knowing what's going to happen from one second to the next. It's not minutes, it's seconds. Suddenly the atmosphere can totally change and your hair stands up on the back of your neck.**'

Karl talked Richard Woolfe, LIVINGtv's director of television, into doing a solo vigil at Fyvie Castle, in Scotland. He remembers: **'My heart was thumping. It was in a room where this woman had been left to die because she had failed to produce an heir. Karl told me I had to stay for 30 minutes and I managed it, but I was really disappointed that nothing happened. The scary bit was beforehand when I was thinking about it and worrying whether I might chicken out on the night. Now I know what it feels like, I think they're all incredible for doing what they do.'**

Fear is Infectious

You'd think it would help to have other team members around who can huddle nearby, providing safety in numbers – but that's not always the case. At some locations, one person's obvious fear has spread to the rest of the team. Cath says: '**When the girls are on our own, shaking in our boots, one scream can set off a chain reaction.**' Watch the Craig y Nos or Jamaica Inn episodes for good examples of places where fear became contagious. And then watch the hilarious incident at the Manor House Restaurant in West Bromwich ...

Derek, Yvette, Jon and Richard Felix went into the ladies' toilet, where there had been many paranormal experiences reported, including sightings of a ghost in medieval costume. They crept in, alert and very tense, when all of a sudden there was a loud hissing noise and something spat at Jon. They all screamed at the tops of their lungs and stampeded for the door. Of course, later investigation showed that there was an air freshener that periodically sprayed fragrance into the air. Everyone was mortified.

At Pendle Hill, in Clitheroe, almost the entire team succumbed to mass fear. Ciaran says: '**It was a most fascinating experiment for a parapsychologist, because there had been a lot of suggestion that there were witches there and there had been talk about hanging. The crew were tired, the atmosphere was dusty; then one person felt a tightening round their throat and once they mentioned it, others began to react too. They started to hyperventilate and a kind of mass hysteria took hold. It affected Jon Gilbert and Stuart, Cath's legs felt weak, Karl felt incredibly cold and Jon Dibley almost collapsed. One by one, they left the hill until it was just Yvette and me, and she was shouting "Hey, we've got no cameramen left here!"'**

Most Scary Moments

Here are a few crew members' 'most scary' experiences, and their personal take on the 'fear factor':

ALEX LYSAGHT 'At the Chough Inn, Richard, Ian Lawman and I went out to investigate a tree where twelve men had been hanged. As we walked down the lane towards it, I felt something rush towards me, then I got a feeling I was being watched. Ian could see a spirit watching us at the bottom of the lane. We left really quickly and when we got back to the car, I was convinced the spirit had got into the car with us. Ian said no, but several spirits were just outside, lots of them, looking in the windows, and I could feel them watching us. That would have to be my "most scary".'

TOR O'NEILL 'I was at the Derby Heritage Centre with Cath, Stuart and Rick and it was my first shoot – I'd never been in a haunted house before. Derek had told us a poltergeist might rap on the wooden panelling and it could cause problems for us. Suddenly the coffee machine came on and I screamed the place down. The total shock and emotion I felt were horrible. Of course, when I look back now, it's embarrassing. People were emailing saying "Who on earth is that crazy woman?"'

DEREK ACORAH 'We've done almost a hundred *Most Haunted* investigations now and I've come across many spirits who have evil intent, but I still say that Godfrey Parks at Brannigan's, back in series 2, was the one that terrified me the most.'

Jon Dibley was seriously shaken by his mini-possession
at Belgrave Hall.

CATH HOWE 'Brannigan's and the House of Detention stand
out as scariest for me. What worries me most is things flying
across the room that could hit you, or being possessed myself.
I also hate it when Derek gets possessed; it doesn't feel safe.
My other scariest experiences were in the cellar at the Black
Swan Inn, when Karl was breaking down the wall. I was almost
literally climbing on Yvette's back, I was huddled so close to her.
Then there's the famous occasion at Greengate Brewery when
I actually peed my pants. No one will let me forget that ... The
first five shows I did, I couldn't go to bed without having all
the lights on in my house, and I even asked my cousin to come
and stay. And I'm afraid there have been times when I've said,
"No, sorry, I can't go down to the cellar on my own."' (There are

descriptions of what happened at the Black Swan and Greengate later in this chapter.)

JON DIBLEY 'It has to be the Ancient Ram Inn, because of what happened to Stuart and because it was actually dangerous. Stuart took a full punch to the stomach, which must be a severe shock to the system. I haven't experienced that extreme and I hope I never do – although at Belgrave Hall, I had that mini-possession during the séance. I was still scared about that the next morning.'

STUART TOREVELL 'Need you ask? I nearly left the show because of what happened at the Ancient Ram Inn. I think I'm getting more scared now than I ever used to, because more stuff is happening to me personally. Greengate Brewery was another one … And I'm still scared of the dark after all this time!'

RACHEL PHILIPS 'I don't like completely pitch-black places, but it all depends how you're feeling on the day. In the basement of Kinnity Castle [in Ireland], it was very scary when the noises seemed to be responding to us and Richard Felix started to cry. Other people seemed scared as well. What would scare me the most would be being on my own and seeing something ugly or creepy, then finding I couldn't get out of the room. I'm a bit of a coward at horror films. I certainly couldn't watch *Poltergeist*.'

RICHARD FELIX 'I'll never forget the feeling of shock and horror at Craig y Nos when I saw a woman's shape lying across my bed in the middle of the night. That was definitely my most scary *Most Haunted* experience. East Kirkby was also frightening because of the whole atmosphere of the place. You were so close to the items [aeroplanes] that people had actually died in. One chap had been cut in half inside a plane. It was like having the car that Eddie Cochrane was killed in or the plane Buddy Holly died in – just a bit close for comfort.'

DAVID WELLS 'I got possessed at Pendle Hill [in Clitheroe]. I felt like a fool because my protection lapsed and a woman got inside. I was scrying at the time [see p. 227] when I suddenly felt very ill, almost vomiting. I can't remember anything that happened after that, but I've watched the footage and I scream like a wolf, pick up the mirror and smash it on the table, then fall onto it. I think the woman was one of the Pendle Witches. I cried my eyes out afterwards, really poured my heart out, and I seriously considered walking away from the show because it was so scary seeing myself doing all those things that I have no memory of.'

YVETTE FIELDING When asked, Yvette always says Greengate Brewery is her 'most scary'. She adds: 'There have been times when I get so scared I can't physically move and I think, "Why am I putting myself through this?" Sometimes I've thought, "That's it!", but I never really mean it – like at Craig y Nos, walking up the stairs hanging onto Richard Felix ... Or in the Workshop at Chatham Dockyard, I was absolutely petrified because it was so black, so dark, and the wind was howling outside, then we heard that dragging noise outside the door, and to this day I don't know what it was. Richard was behind me, but I felt so vulnerable, as if something was there, and it was a horrible feeling ... Getting lost is very common, especially in the bigger places like the Station Hotel [in Dudley], and it adds to the terror.'

Yvette seems to get braver with each series, often challenging herself to stay alone in rooms or walk along spooky corridors. Think back to the first series, when she tried to spend five minutes alone in the most haunted room at the Red Lion Pub in Avebury but had to flee when she felt something tickling her hair. Remember how she challenged herself over and over again to do a vigil in that corridor at Levens Hall but kept freaking out when the door seemed to shut on its own. But by series 4, she had no problem staying alone in the most haunted room at Tutbury Castle, which has had to be closed to the public because so many people were passing out in there. And think of Yvette standing up to the spirit that had possessed Derek in Owlpen Manor, or teasing the spirit during table-tipping at Maes Artro, and resisting the group panic on Pendle Hill ... She's definitely much tougher than she used to be.

Karl, of course, has been the bravest all the way through the series, although he says he does get frightened at times. Like in the dungeon at Chillingham Castle, when he was doing one of his lone vigils, or when he went back to the Chatham Dockyard Workshop on his own after the others had heard that dragging noise. But we're more used to seeing Karl pulling off his courageous stunts – such as the famous occasion when he climbed through a wall in the creepy basement of the Black Swan Inn.

Uri Geller at the Black Swan Inn.

The Black Swan Inn, Wiltshire

Uri Geller, world-renowned psychic, joined the team for their night at the Black Swan, in Devizes, and he and Derek worked in a complementary way that helped to clarify the story of some of the gruesome events that seemed to have taken place there. Early on, Derek claimed to feel that there were **'things that should be unearthed, that will have a major, major significance in the investigation. They need to break open and go into another chamber to find remnants of the past.'**

As they went down to the cellar, both men exclaimed at the negative energy they could feel. **'Like a cold wind, dense with death,'** said Uri. Soon Derek's chest began to feel tight as he picked up the energies of one individual. Ciaran's EMF meter suddenly flicked up to the maximum as Derek described what he could feel: a young girl who had had her throat slit, with blood gushing from it, yet she was still alive and crawling across the room when a man put his foot on her back to stop her. Uri thought there might be more than one spirit there: **'I feel a small mass grave; the walls, bricks, mortar are drenched in blood. Gruesome things were done here.'**

What the two psychics didn't know is that there is said to be a tunnel in the cellar, just near the area where they felt the strong negative energies. Five years before, a local historian had removed a couple of bricks from the wall, to try to see what lay behind it, and it was after that that the paranormal activity in the hotel began, as if he had disturbed some spirits who lay behind. Uri was nervous when he put his hand through the gap in the wall where the bricks had been removed. **'I'm afraid something will grab it,'** he said, then reported that it was as cold as the inside of a refrigerator back there.

So what did Karl do? After consultation with the owner, he decided to break down a section of the 300-year-old wall to see if he could solve the mystery. He removed a few bricks to enlarge the hole and then, to gasps from the onlookers, he began to crawl through the aperture.

'Are you *really* going in there?' Uri asked, horrified.

'I had to go through,' Karl recalls. **'I love it! If I move these bricks, maybe there'll be something in there, some dead bodies or whatever,**

Karl crawling through the hole.

or maybe there'll be proof of paranormal activity. There's got to be a link, because the haunting started when a brick was removed.'

Inside, Karl found that he was in a gap between two walls, where it was very difficult to breathe. There was a lot of swearing as he tried to film in the enclosed space. Before long, he had passed out two pieces of bone that were identified by Uri as a human rib and part of a left foot.

Karl set to work on the second wall that lay behind the first one, although he was at a very odd angle and terribly cramped for swinging a hammer. He began to feel depressed, as though something didn't want him to get through. And it seems that was the case, because the more he chipped away at the second wall, the more he realized that it had been very carefully constructed to prevent anyone getting through.

The semicircle of brickwork was arranged so that you would have to pull bricks towards you to get them out, but there was no room to do so in that tiny cavity. Whoever constructed it must have been very keen to stop anyone seeing the other side. Karl managed to dislodge a few bricks and peer through, but all he could see on the other side were piles of rubble. Disheartened, he came out of the wall cavity – but we wait with interest to see what will happen if the owner decides to have those walls professionally demolished.

The team decided to do a last vigil in the cellar in case any spirits had been roused by the bricks Karl had removed. Soon they saw a very clear light anomaly that Uri said was a spirit. Yvette got very scared,

GUESSING GAMES

Eagle-eyed viewers may have noticed some odd symbols drawn in pen on the palm of Uri Geller's hand while they were down in the cellar. Karl explains what they were. 'He drew a pattern and I had to guess what it was. It's not too difficult a trick. If someone says "pick two shapes", 80 per cent of people will say "triangle and circle", and if you ask them to come up with a two-digit number, most will answer 37. However, Uri impressed the living hell out of me years ago, when I was filming a show he was on. He took a Yale key from one of the riggers and just touched it lightly and it started to bend. It was still bending when he put it back in the rigger's hand. Now you *cannot* bend a metal object like that. I certainly can't explain it.'

and they all sensed some kind of presence in there. Suddenly, something was thrown from the ceiling – a stone, or perhaps something softer. Uri seemed quite taken aback. '**I am now much more convinced there is a presence here,**' he said. '**It gives us a glimpse into the beyond.**'

Yvette later said that Uri seemed '**scared to death in that cellar – really terrified**'.

To test your own courage, ask yourself one question, honestly: would *you* have climbed through the hole in that cellar wall? Would you?

Greengate Brewery, Manchester

Aside from Karl, Stuart is the team member most likely to wander off on his own, in the dead of night, to the parts of a location said to have the most paranormal activity. In Greengate Brewery, his intrepid explorations were to provide the team with one of their most memorable pieces of footage to date. But why did everyone get so spooked there? And why did Yvette rate it her '**most scary of all**'?

First of all, the baseline tests presented some new challenges. The crew had never filmed in a brewery before but they soon came to realize that tapping sounds can come from airlocks in pipes, a hissing noise can be gas escaping from a barrel, pipework can transmit sound from one end of the building to another and, as in many other larger premises they'd filmed, it was easy to get lost. There was one more unpleasant element they had to get used to. '**That place just stank of beer,**' says Jon Dibley, '**The smell stayed with me for days afterwards.**'

On an early walkabout, Yvette, Tom O'Carroll, Derek and Phil Whyman were startled by the clear sound of beer barrels clanking against each other five times. Yvette reproduced the noise downstairs in the Barrel Room and they all agreed that was what they had heard … but no one had actually been there to clank the barrels together. Jon and Stuart did manage to track down the source of a regular tapping noise that had been freaking them out – it was a type of electric meter in a small alcove in the basement.

When the team split up into groups to do their night vigils, they were all a bit apprehensive – and with good reason:

- Soon after Cath and Suzanne Vinton arrived in the Brewing Room, Cath felt something touching her back and then she heard a footstep right next to her. It's hard to think of a *Most Haunted* show where Cath has appeared more terrified. '**Oh it was horrible**,' she says. '**I could hear footsteps and noises and the light went on and off, but there was no one there. That's when I wet myself – not completely, though, only a little bit.**'

- Down in the basement, Karl and Yvette challenged any spirit to make itself known. All of a sudden, something dropped down from the pipes behind them, making a loud clatter. '**There's something there,**' Yvette hissed to Karl. '**What frightens me more than anything else is the thought that they're trying to hit you, leaving me on my own.**' After a few more thumping noises, she'd had enough. '**I want to go. Please. I'm sorry, it's just too scary.**' Looking back, she tried to figure out what could have caused things to fall to the floor. '**There was a clunk like something being** thrown and hitting against metal. Karl had an arm round me and his other hand on the camera and there was no one else in the room, so who was throwing that stuff? I've had letters and emails from people who've visited Greengate and the same thing happened to them. There was a long, dark tunnel to get out and I was shaking, a mess, claustrophobic. I've never heard anything as loud as that before.' Karl went back on his own to look for Stuart and Jon, but the spooky noises drove even him back upstairs again to find company.

- Up in the Attic Filing Room, a tall cloaked figure had often been seen wandering amongst the rows of files – and sometimes right through them. Employee Diane Bowden described a shadowy figure she saw once. 'It went right through me lever-arch files,' she said. Derek was joined up there by David, Jon, Richard, Phil and Tom. Derek and David identified a lonely, desperate, shameful figure with a scar on his face. David felt a tap on his back, and then a tall, shelved cupboard behind Derek began to rock backwards and forwards as if it was going to topple over. You can see from the footage that Derek hasn't touched it, but the shot isn't quite wide enough to see what anyone else is doing. Derek knows what he believes: 'There was a spirit who wanted to come inside me, but I wouldn't let him. He moved past David's shoulder, then I felt a rush behind me and the cupboard moved. Now that was one heavy piece of material; it took a strong person to budge it.' Stuart and Jon think someone trod on a loose floorboard that set it rocking, but Derek and David remain convinced the cupboard was pushed by a cloaked figure they both independently named as 'Thomas'.

It was at 4 a.m. that Stuart decided to challenge himself to spend half an hour down in the basement Barrel Room that had freaked Yvette out so badly. **'We're not told where to go, we can go off wherever we want to, but going somewhere on your own is a big thing. Especially at Greengate, because there were all those tapping noises from the air-assisted pumps. We might look like we're not bothered, but we are.'** He took a lock-off camera and a hand-held camcorder and stood in the middle of the room, asking **'Are you a nasty spirit or a nice spirit? I don't wish you any harm … Would you like to show yourself? Anybody there? Who's that? … Oh, fucking hell!'**

Here's what happened, in Stuart's words: **'First I saw a dark shape up the corridor and thought there must be someone up there, but no one replied, and we can't mess about with each other on this job – we have to take it seriously. The only two [brewery] staff on the site were security guards at the front entrance. There was lots of condensation on the cold pipes that was dripping down the channel. Then I heard the barrels clanging. They were stacked at the far end and would have to be physically picked up and placed on the tracks. The beam on the night-vision only covers about 3 metres but I directed the camera up there, and then I called Alex and said, "The shit's hitting the fan. Send Karl down here right now, send a medium, send as many people as possible." I wanted nothing more than to run off, but the way out was in the direction the barrel was coming from. The only thing that got me through was thinking "This is a television programme and if**

What caused the barrel to move in Greengate Brewery?

I were sat at home, I'd want to see this". The barrel came trundling all the way down the track then kept rolling back and forth on a slight indent at the end of the line and I kept filming. There was no human being there. It has to be paranormal.'

Dave Nuttall, marketing manager at Greengate Brewery, explained that the barrels couldn't possibly roll down the track on their own. They need a push to get started and, as far as he knew, the run had been empty at the start of the night. Seemingly, there have been a couple of other reports of staff getting a terrible shock when barrels roll on their own. Even renowned sceptic Matthew Smith found this 'quite convincing evidence of paranormal activity'.

So there were several factors that made this a memorably scary night for the team: the unfamiliarity of the surroundings, the odd acoustics and inexplicable noises; but more than this, everyone felt a real sense of presence. All these combined to create a very tense atmosphere that gets Greengate Brewery into most of the crew's Top Five All-Time Most Scary Investigations.

CHAPTER 17

Developing Your Psychic Abilities

We all get instincts about people on first meeting or pick up atmospheres in buildings we've never visited before. Instinct might sway you to buy one house rather than another, even though the price, number of rooms and location were all similar. You would opt for the one that had a 'good feeling' about it.

Recent scientific research has seemed to confirm the existence of a kind of sixth sense that picks up mood and atmosphere. Researchers found that blind people could sense the emotions of someone else in a room with them without a word being uttered, and those who are not blind can back their hunches with visual clues as well.

Derek advises that if you want to open yourself to the spirit world, you should '**use a professional to guide you, and be prepared for a lot of hard work. Nothing comes easy. You can't do it overnight, and you should hear warning bells if anyone suggests you can. Look for tried-and-tested teachers who've seen hundreds of thousands of spirits themselves. The psychic profession is like a beautiful barrel, full of gorgeous fruits – but one rotten one can make them all look rotten.**'

'Being psychic is not a gift,' says David. 'It's a talent we all have that you can choose to train. To work professionally you should find good training, such as Buddhic, Kabbalistic or through the spiritualist church. But if you just want to develop your psychic abilities in everyday life, switch the TV off, stop reading newspapers, get outside and walk and start noticing the stuff you have never observed

CONTACTING LOVED ONES

David says: 'When you have lost someone close, you naturally have communication with them in the spirit world, but most people tend to dismiss it as their imagination. They're waiting to hear their loved one's voice, but that's not what happens; you hear your own voice with their words. To test it out, the best thing to do is say "If it is you, please tell me something that I'll have to go and ask another relative to prove". Then write it down before you seek the proof.' However, don't think you can 'command' spirits to respond when you want them to, or that they love you any less if they don't. David explains: 'They have things to do up there. They're still busy. They work with children, they help adults across; when there's a disaster they help people to understand and pull them across. They still work, doing something they want to do, and it can be the opposite of what they did in life.'

before. Meditate daily – this is the single biggest thing – and you will learn to listen on a different level.'

The *Most Haunted* team get hundreds of letters a year from viewers who believe their houses are haunted, telling of their paranormal experiences and asking advice. Derek's advice would always be to go to a medium or a spiritualist church rather than trying to deal with the spirit youself. He says: **'Word of mouth is the best way to find a medium. The best ones don't advertise, their reputation goes before them. Someone on your life's path will guide you in the right direction.'**

Karl is not as cautious as Derek, because he's curious and drawn to investigate things himself. **'Set up your own trigger object on a surface covered with flour,'** he suggests. **'Dictaphones don't cost a great deal and if you get a voice-activated one, you won't have hours of blank tape. Infrared surveillance cameras aren't too expensive and give you eight hours of long-play recording, so they could be left on all night.'**

Throughout the book, there have been descriptions of methods the team have used to try to communicate with spirits – including séances, ouija boards, table-tipping, glass-moving, psychometry and EVP. In this chapter, there are some other methods of communication that members of the *Most Haunted* team have tried at one time or another and some theories they have explored. If you decide to try any of them yourself, be wary. Remember that Derek and David don't think you should try any communication techniques yourself without the professional guidance of an experienced medium.

Scrying

This is where you stare into a mirror or reflective surface to see if you can see a spirit in the reflection. In Ancient Greece, they used to look into a pool of blood to see if the spirit was there. Ian Lawman often uses this technique (although not with blood): **'I sprinkle water over the top of a mirror so it trickles down causing a blurred effect, and the energy from the water attracts spirits.'**

At Ordsall Hall, in Manchester, Ian, Ciaran, Tom and Yvette tried scrying with water poured down a mirror. At first they saw an old face, with wrinkles and deep-set eyes, which went blank and then changed shape. Yvette saw her own face transfigurating, then disappearing, and she became quite freaked out about it. Ian's face seemed to have a long moustache, then his head disappeared. It was a very emotional experience, but Ciaran doesn't rate it as evidence of the paranormal. **'They were in a dark room, staring for a long time, and your eyes begin to play tricks, losing depth perception.'**

Karl also doesn't rate scrying: **'I think it's an optical illusion. If you stare at anything for long enough, for example, if you write a word enough times, it doesn't look right. So if you stare in a mirror, things will start appearing.'**

But look back at the image Yvette captured in the mirror at the Jamaica Inn (p. 101). Was she just imagining a figure in there? Could *you* see it?

Automatic Writing

The team have tried this at a few locations, including Derby Gaol, but they've never come up with anything significant. The idea is that you sit with a pen and paper and ask a spirit to write through you, using your hand. Derek says he has seen someone write pages and pages of intricate, articulate words way beyond their intellectual capacity, but team members have only come up with meaningless scribbles.

Automatism can be used with virtually any creative activity, including painting, playing a musical instrument, dancing and sculpting. Psychic researchers generally explain the results as coming from depths of knowledge or talent that the person has forgotten or repressed, rather than from a spirit entity, but why not try it yourself? Just sit down with a pen and a piece of paper, preferably in the dark, then empty your conscious mind and see what comes through.

Dowsing

Richard and Yvette are always arguing about this. She is convinced that involuntary micro-muscular spasms or the pulse in your fingertips cause dowsing rods to move, but Richard has quite another take on it. Here are his views, in his own words: '**They used to teach African and Aborigine children how to find their way home by dowsing. They would walk round and round in a circle thinking of their mum and dad, and then set off. We don't use those powers any more because we have telephones, but they can still work. You can dowse for anything you want to find and, if you are determined enough, you will find it. Some** people use hazel twigs, but I use two bent metal coathangers and a dowsing crystal. I don't know exactly how it works, but it's definitely not my hand twitching. I think it could be a spirit controlling the mind or some kind of psychokinesis. But if you ask questions, you get genuine answers, as if there is a soul trying to communicate. You can also try asking questions with a crystal on a chain – yes is clockwise and no is anticlockwise. To tell if there's energy around, place your hand on a piece of stone and watch the crystal start to vibrate. Now take your hand off and it stops vibrating. I find it quite astonishing!'

They don't often feature Richard and his rods on the show, but he's had some interesting results with *Most Haunted*, such as finding the hidden tunnel at Moresby Hall, in Cumbria.

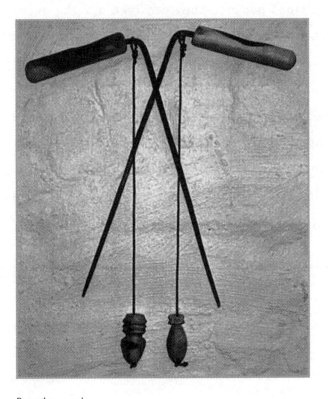

Dowsing rods.

LEY LINES

Richard is the member of the team who has the most interest in ley lines, which he describes as ancient lines of communication. 'Prehistoric people had more space in their brains, because they weren't full of pin numbers and all the other stuff we have to remember nowadays. They used to communicate via telepathy, and those lines of communication followed particular tracks through the fields which, as the years went on, became roads. All the ancient monuments, like Avebury and Stonehenge, are in straight lines. There's a possibility that spirits travel along ley lines because they can feed off the energy. At places where lots of ley lines meet and cross each other, you are likely to find more spirits.' According to Richard, the Ancient Ram Inn is at a junction of different ley lines, so maybe that goes some way towards explaining the extraordinarily dramatic night the team had there. On the other hand, as Ciaran points out, most places have some kind of ley line connection because there are so many of them criss-crossing the country.

Yvette among the prehistoric Avebury Stones.

Past-Life Regression

One of David's specialities is to use creative visualizations to take people back on a journey to their previous incarnations. He says this helps them to understand who their spirit guide is and what their purpose might be in this present lifetime, so therefore what they have to learn. **'Most people have probably had hundreds of incarnations already,'** he explains. **'Your soul age depends on how much learning you've taken on along the way. Old age is in the 90s; I'm currently 38, but there's someone in my Kabbalah group who's just 7. I found out that my mum was my daughter in a previous life and my sister has been my wife. People who try regression find it a remarkable, life-changing experience that helps them to understand what their life is about.'**

Yvette has misgivings about past-life regression: '**My feeling is you're not supposed to know that stuff. I wouldn't do it personally.** [She laughs.] **Not unless someone offered me a lot of money to do it!'** However, Yvette did set David a challenge at Greengate Brewery, when she asked if he could use his skills to find out about previous uses of the building. He couldn't regress the brewery directly but he decided to use an individual team member – Tom O'Carroll – and regress the building around him.

Although Tom is a sceptic, he found himself describing the room they were standing in as a tiny cottage, and he picked up on several 'astral beings'. '**One of them was my grandmother,**' David chuckles. '**She's always poking her nose in.'** Tom describes what he felt: '**David opened up a psychic pathway for me and took me back to what I thought was 1836. I really did "see" people and wonder if what I experienced is what mediums get whenever they open up. It was a lovely experience.'**

Astrology and Tarot

When David first approached a Kabbalah teacher to try to make sense of all the spirits he was seeing and hearing in his everyday life, the teacher advised him to learn astrology first because it's grounding. '**Then she suggested Kabbalah, a system for understanding your place in the universe, and I loved it immediately. Next I studied past-life therapy and then tarot cards. All the different systems merge together to unfold your soul.**' David uses the energies of tarot and astrology in his private readings to help refine and clarify the messages.

Karl is a fan: 'David did Yvette's chart and it's been 100 per cent correct to the week, so that's changed my idea of astrology. We might use it on the show, for example, if the planets indicated there could be more spiritual activity on one night than another. We haven't used tarot yet but we probably will, because we aim to investigate everything.'

Try any of the techniques described if you want to sharpen your own psychic abilities, or just use them in everyday life. When the phone rings, try to predict who it will be before you lift the receiver. When you walk into a room with other people in it, try to sense the general mood before a word is spoken. Visit old houses without reading about their history beforehand and decide whether you get a good feeling or not, if there are any parts of the building that make you feel odd or if you can get a sense of previous occupants. Try to psychometrize any antiques you come across. Learn how to meditate and practise regularly.

Many of the locations in which the *Most Haunted* team have filmed are open to the public, so you could go along and see how your experience compares with theirs (you'll find a full list at the back of the book). And if you can find a group of like-minded people to explore with, you may find – as the crew have done – that things get more and more interesting.

CHAPTER 18

Will They
Prove It?

Derek is convinced that they will manage to film a full spirit manifestation on *Most Haunted* some day, but Karl is not so sure. **'It seems to me that the best weapon against a ghost is a camera – they never show themselves when you're holding one! If you see it through a camera, you've caught it, and life isn't that good. Besides, even if we got one, people would say we'd faked it. If we do catch anything, I'll hand over the unedited rushes to an independent expert for verification. But it's that old catch-22 situation: to a believer, no proof is necessary, and to a non-believer, no proof is possible.'**

What would constitute proof positive of the existence of ghosts? Ciaran's approach to any strange noises or experiences on the show is to run through every possible natural cause first, to see whether he can discount them. Whenever there's a spooky noise or some spirit lights or ghostly whispers, you won't find Ciaran running away; he runs towards them, taking readings to try to build up a case. When someone has had an odd experience, he questions them at length about what happened, how they felt, whether they were tired at the time and so on.

He explains: '**I want to be able to show on camera that there's no natural explanation if, for example, things are being thrown in a darkened room. Is something falling from the ceiling? Is it a bat? A bird? An animal? Or is someone messing about? The proof I am looking for would be if you had a video camera in a securely locked-off room and captured a full-bodied apparition or some clear poltergeist activity ... So far, lots of things have happened on** *Most Haunted* **that I have no explanation for, but nothing I'd call proof.**'

It can be frustrating for the others that Ciaran's basic approach is to try to discount things first. Ian Lawman quips: '**I could materialize Ciaran's grandfather in front of him and he'd still want more proof.**'

Ciaran responds: '**If he materialized my grandfather, that would prove it to me, but I'd still have to convince the scientific world and personal testimony wouldn't do.**'

Richard comes in at the opposite side of the equation: '**While Ciaran is trying to disprove, I want to prove that the dead do return. For example, if someone sees a ghostly monk on a property but there seems no logical explanation why a monk would be there, I'll run off and recheck the history of the building and maybe I'll find that the foundation stones were part of an old monastery. But I'm still aware how difficult it would be to convince the world. Even if we filled the Albert Hall with 4,000 people and produced a full-blown materialization of a ghost onstage, the 50 billion TV viewers sitting at home round the world would be sceptical ... You have to remember that 500 years ago, we believed that if we sailed too far out on the ocean, we would fall off the edge of the earth. The proof of ghosts is individual, and it comes from being there and seeing it for yourself.**'

CIARAN'S UNUSUAL CAREER

'I was always fascinated by ghost stories,' he says, 'and wanted to make it my career. When I was 16 or 17, I saw the film *Ghostbusters*, which mentions a parapsychology department at Columbia University, so I called them. They said, "Oh, not another caller! We'll direct you to someone who *does* have courses." I went to Washington College in Maryland, where I did a thesis in parapsychology, then came back to the UK and did a Masters in investigative psychology - about the way psychics can assist detectives in criminal cases. Then I got the chance to do my PhD testing mediums and psychics and I was awarded the research post at Liverpool Hope. There's a move nowadays for parapsychologists to come out of the lab and do investigations in the real world, so when I got the call from *Most Haunted*, I jumped at the chance. It's a great opportunity for me to explore paranormal beliefs.'
To find out more about his research, visit his website www.theparapsychologist.com.

It seems that more people have experienced individual proof now than they had 50 years ago. According to a recent ICM survey that was published in the *Sunday Times*, 42 per cent of us think ghosts exist, whereas only 33 per cent thought so in 1954. There are increasing numbers of academics in university departments conducting studies into paranormal phenomena, including Ciaran's department at Liverpool

Hope University; the Koestler Parapsychology Unit at Edinburgh University; Goldsmiths College in London; Nottingham University; and a couple of others. The Society for Psychical Research funds a number of investigations into hauntings and poltergeist activity, and Ciaran has done some work for them.

Professor Bernard Carr of Queen Mary, University of London, is a mathematics professor as well as vice-president of the Society for Psychical Research, just one of many respected academics with an interest in parapsychology. '**I don't think all apparitions are just creations of the mind,**' he says in the same *Sunday Times* article. '**For example, there are collective cases where several people see the same apparition at the same or different times. There are also cases where the apparition conveys information that was unknown at the time but subsequently verified. Although we don't fully understand these phenomena, scientists should investigate them.**'

What Next?

So what next for *Most Haunted*? Each series seems to be more dramatic than the last as the team continue working together and getting more and more psychically open. The more experiences an individual has, the more they can expect to happen in future. For example, in early series, very little happened to Stuart, but he seems to have crossed some kind of psychic threshold and spirits make a beeline for him now. He says: '**I don't know why they sometimes come to me instead of Derek. Maybe I'm more open now, and whether that has anything to do with what happened at the Ancient Ram Inn or not, I don't know. But I'm** definitely more scared than I used to be when we walk into a new place.'

David has begun questioning spirits in visitation about their after-death experiences. He asks: **'Did you see a white light as you left the physical body? What age did you die? What age are you over there, and what age do you feel? Did you meet any relations on the other side? Have you met any angels? Do you have work to do over there? Do you eat and drink?'** Watch out for his findings in future series …

Yvette would like to be able to spend more time at the most scary properties. **'I would love to spend a week, two weeks, in the Ram Inn, the Golden Fleece, Greengate Brewery or Maes Artro, and do a really thorough investigation using the thermal-imaging camera and all the new equipment we have now that we didn't have on earlier series. That would be amazing – but we just don't have the time.'**

'The subject will always attract interest,' says Karl, **'and the show itself will go on and on, even if some of the team change over the years. I'm not going anywhere. To me, this is the best job in the world: to spend all night in disused underground stations, or in a condemned man's cell at Derby Gaol or in a morgue – it's just superb! You'll never get a chance to do that again, and I don't want to miss a second of it.'**

Neither do we, Karl!

Appendix:
Most Haunted Locations

Series 1

Chillingham Castle, Northumberland

The Ostrich Inn, Buckinghamshire

Souter Lighthouse, Tyne and Wear

Avebury Stones, Wiltshire

Red Lion Pub, Avebury

Culzean Castle, Ayrshire

Derby Gaol

Athelhampton Hall, Dorset

Aldwych Underground Station, London

Treasure Holt, Colchester

The Mermaid Inn, East Sussex

Blackpool Pleasure Beach, Lancashire

Drury Lane Theatre, London

Charnock Hall, Preston

Leap Castle, County Offaly, Ireland

Charleville Forest Castle, County Offaly, Ireland

Michelham Priory, East Sussex

One-hour Special: Levens Hall, Cumbria

Series 2

The Bell Inn, Derby

Lafferty's Pub, Derby

The Heritage Centre, Derby

Brannigan's Nightclub, Manchester

Tutbury Castle, Staffordshire

The Skirrid Inn, Gwent

Llanciaich Fawr Manor House, West Glamorgan

The Station Hotel, Dudley

Pengersick Castle, Cornwall

The House of Detention, London

The Clockhouse, Surrey

Caesars Nightclub, London

Series 3

RAF East Kirkby, Lincolnshire

Moresby Hall, Cumbria

Edinburgh Vaults

Leith Hall, Aberdeenshire

The Schooner Hotel, Northumberland

Aberglasney House, Dyfed

Fitz Manor, Shropshire

The Muckleburgh Collection, Norfolk

Galleries of Justice, Nottingham

Tamworth Castle, Staffordshire

Celebrity Special: Belgrave Hall, Leicester
(with Vic Reeves and Nancy Sorrell)

Series 4

The Hell Fire Caves, Buckinghamshire

Craig y Nos, Powys

Jamaica Inn, Cornwall

The Wellington Hotel, Cornwall

Owlpen Manor, Gloucestershire

The Manor House Hotel, County Durham

Croxteth Hall, Liverpool

Chatham Dockyard/Commissioner's House, Kent

Mary King's Close, Edinburgh

Greengate Brewery, Manchester

Guildhall, Leicester

The Manor House Restaurant, West Bromwich

Series 5

Kinnity Castle, County Offaly, Ireland

Castle Leslie, County Monaghan, Ireland

Kasteel Doorwerth, Netherlands

Kasteel Ammersoyen, Netherlands

Sandbach Old Hall, Cheshire (with Gaby Roslin)

The Chough Inn, Somerset (with Dr David Bull)

The Black Swan, Wiltshire (with Uri Geller)

Ordsall Hall, Manchester

Samlesbury Hall, Preston

Oldham Coliseum, Greater Manchester

Pleasley Vale Mills, Mansfield

Bodelwyddan Castle, Clwyd

Annesley Hall, Nottinghamshire

The Ancient Ram Inn, Gloucestershire

Series 6

The Golden Fleece, York (with Scott Mills, Radio1)

The Ghost House, Worksop

Dalston Hall, Carlisle

Bodmin Jail, Cornwall

Prideaux Place, Cornwall

Lower Wellhead Farm, Lancashire

Tynedale Farm, Lancashire

Petty France Manor House, Gloucestershire

Somerleyton Hall, Norfolk

London Dungeons

Arreton Manor, Isle of Wight

Appledurcombe House, Isle of Wight

Fyvie Castle, Aberdeenshire

Craigievar, Aberdeenshire

USA Locations

Whaley House, California

RMS *Queen Mary*, California

American Legion

You can order *Most Haunted* DVDs from **www.livingtv.co.uk/shop**

Notes

for you to make on your house